IN SEARCH OF THE JAGUAR

IN SEARCH OF THE JAGUAR

Stan Steiner

Times BOOKS

Published by TIMES BOOKS, a division of Quadrangle/The New York Times Book Co., Inc.
Three Park Avenue, New York, N.Y. 10016

Published simultaneously in Canada by Fitzhenry & Whiteside, Ltd., Toronto.

Library of Congress Cataloging in Publication Data

Steiner, Stan.
In search of the jaguar.

1. Venezuela—Politics and government—1935– —Addresses, essays, lectures. 2. Venezuela— Economic conditions—1918– —Addresses, essays, lectures. I. Title.

JL3831.S73 1979 320.9'87'063 78-24245

ISBN 0-8129-0805-8

Manufactured in the United States of America

To the memory of
Stephen Polgar
who shared my interest in and my devotion
to the fate of the peoples and nations
of the Third World

Contents

Acknowledgments

May I offer my appreciation and my gratitude to my friends and colleagues in Venezuela who offered me their hands and hearts and thoughts in the writing of this book:

Desmond Abraham
Martha Sequera
Fatima Silva
Liesel Gras
Patrick Milanese
Larry Vincent
David Getter
Fernando Gonzales
Jose Alirio Gonzales
Manuel Vargas

And God Said

And God said: I will create a perfect country which has everything that human beings desire. That has gold and diamonds, petroleum and iron, great rivers and mountains, tropical forests and flowers, idyllic beaches and villages, and the most beautiful women in the world.

And then God was asked: Who shall live in this perfect country?

And God said: The most imperfect people in the world—whomI shall call Venezuelans.

This parable is said to have been told by don Juan Pablo Pérez Alfonzo, the patron of the oil industry of Venezuela and the founder of OPEC.

The Candles of the Wise Old Man

"My garden is my world," the old man says.

The garden is his Noah's Ark for tropical flowers and trees. And the old man walks among his plants, calling each by name, as fondly as a proud grandfather. It is as though he is seeking in his own way to preserve a natural world, here in his garden, that is dying in the world outside—much as the biblical Noah did. For the old man, too, has foreseen the coming of the flood.

Of the city of Caracas that surrounds his garden, he says, "It shall fall in a great catastrophe," though many say the petroleum wealth which has built the city is largely of his own creation. The old man in the garden is the founder of OPEC.

"Now I am confined to my garden and my house," he says. "It is a voluntary confinement. I will not go into the city."

In the garden, in the suburbs, on the edge of the city, at the foot of the mountain, his garden wall is an embattled rampart that has been breached. And the old man is engaged in a battle with the inevitability of urban growth which each day grows closer and noisier; it has surmounted his garden wall. He is in a strategic retreat. But he adamantly refuses to surrender to the world he has helped create.

The old man has the look of a seventy-five-year-old cherub, with his gentle face and playful eyes. But, as always, looks may be disarmingly deceiving. He is a tough old warrior. In his easygoing manner there is only the slightest hint of his power, for his policies have changed the political balance of the contemporary world. Nor is there any hint, at all, of his apocalyptical beliefs that the world that he helped create may now be doomed.

Don Juan Pablo Pérez Alfonzo is the old man's name. He is not only the founder of OPEC, but also the father of the nationalization of the petroleum resources of the Third World.

Is his garden just an old man's affectation? A pretense at wisdom? Some say that he is a fool. Some say that he has become senile. The aged emperor who delights in playing the court jester for his own amusement.

On the morning that I visit him in his garden, he is sitting beneath an arbor of tropical vines. He has to stay out of the sun, he laughs, and points to his impishly bald head. Don Juan Pablo is a small man and his large, bald head is impressive; it gives him a somewhat pixyish appearance.

In the cool shadows the city seems far away. So we sit as one should in a morning garden and try to talk of polite pleasantries. But, there is no escaping from the city. The silence of the sky is shattered by the drone of helicopters which fly back and forth above our heads, and the staccato whirl of the propellers drowns out our conversation.

Don Juan Pablo winces: "The noise is terrible. All day they come and go, for they bring building materials for building electric towers on the mountain. So they destroy the landscape."

"Ah, I can't hear," he says. "Let us go inside the house."

The small mansion in which he and his family live, he designed and built by himself. It is an unpretentious home, full of familial paintings and comfortable old furniture.

In this gracious house Don Juan Pablo uses as little electricity as he can. Often, in the evening, he will light candles to save energy. The founder of OPEC sitting in the flickering glow of candlelight; it is an image of himself that he obviously finds pleasing, both because of his conservationist ideas and because it seems so delightfully mischievous a paradox.

And so I say to him: "Is it true that when the sunset comes you tell your guests to go home?"

He says: "To my thinking, it should be considered a cosmic crime, the way we use energy resources. Now, I have said I will be happy to receive visitors from sunrise to sunset, because I do not want to use electricity. Sometimes when I have a visitor I say to him: The sun has already gone. So you should go.

"I remember the time I was vacationing in a cabin where there were no electric lights. There was electricity only in Caracas then. Not in the country. And we used gas lights. So, when I was in jail, during the dictatorship, I was not so uncomfortable not having electric lights in my cell. In my cell I had a kerosene lamp that I kept so that I could read from time to time. That was much better than it is nowadays. And it was less complicated, and less wasteful."

And so I say to him: "Are we going back to the days before we had electricity?"

He says: "Yes, I think that will come. *Porque*? Why? Because we cannot keep on going the way we are. It worries me that most of the advanced industrial nations still think they can use more and more energy, when there is less and less.

"In the use of energy there are two roads. We have taken the wrong road. The right road would be to use renewable energy, such as wood. If you can take care of the forests and use wood for energy, then you would have renewable energy that would last forever. That sounds so simple and logical. That is because it is.

"Consider the use of bicycles. I think the bicycle is the most important instrument of transportation that man has because if you transport one gram, one kilometer, with your own body, it uses up only fifteen calories. And if you go by car it costs many more calories from the earth. So if you project the use of energy by a motor car and by man, then man has a better form of transportation in his own body, on a bicycle."

And I say to him: "That seems like a strange philosophy for the man who founded OPEC. If you feel that way why did you found OPEC? Hasn't OPEC increased the consumption of energy, especially energy used by cars?"

He says: "Still, I think OPEC is a good instrument for the Third World. It hasn't been used properly. As I see it, this could become the bicycle by which we in the Third World may stop the wastage of our energy resources. That was how I envisioned OPEC when I had thought of it, back in 1946, when I was Minister of Mines. Most people see OPEC as a way to raise oil prices, but I see it as a way to lower the use of energy.

"My first contact was made in Washington with the Ambassador of Iran. Later he became Prime Minister. I thought the only way we could stop the exploitation of the multinational companies was for us to get together. The

Iranians were agreeable and invited us to visit them. And then Iran began to nationalize their oil during the regime of Mossadegh, in 1947. But then their government was overthrown (perhaps by the CIA). In some ways it was our fault. The Iranians had begun to ask the oil companies for conditions similiar to those we were establishing in Venezuela.

"I was in Washington when Mossadegh came to the United Nations and started crying, as he often did. And I remember I thought that if we could have helped him, we would have helped all of humanity. Even then we were beginning to think of the need for controlling the use of our natural resources.

"Not having been able to establish OPEC in the 1940s, but having to wait until the 1960s, has damaged the future of the whole world. The consuming countries have become so dependent on imported oil that they no longer may wish to think of changing their ways. And now the role of OPEC has really disappeared. The United States has, in a way, conquered Saudi Arabia and they manage the Shah of Iran. So, OPEC has lost its purpose."

And I say to him: "Most of the ministers in the cabinet and the oil men do not see OPEC as you do. If you are their teacher, why haven't they learned the lesson you have tried to teach them?"

He says: "They are afraid. They don't want to look around because they are afraid to see what is going on as the result of the oil boom. If they look around they will see abandoned, hungry children. So, they put a cover over their eyes and try not to feel anything. It is as if the teachers in the schools of government grew tired of their children.

"Politics is politics. That is why I was very glad when I was sent to jail under the dictatorship. Because the burden of my office was taken from me. Now that I am out of the circus, I can say what I think."

And I say to him: "You seem pessimistic about Venezuela's future."

He says: "I am still optimistic. Many times change comes suddenly. But, I think what OPEC could have been and still can be in the future."

And I say to him: "What change?"

He says: "Civilizations fall. And that always will be so, until man learns not to live in such civilizations. One can improve one's life, but not in a way that destroys one's surrounding. Then you destroy your life. Then there has to be a great catastrophe. And then these civilizations disappear. Sometimes civilizations do destroy themselves. They die. They die. They die.

"I don't know what will happen in the future. Maybe there will be another earthquake here. Caracas is in an earthquake zone and it has happened once before, so it may happen again, and destroy Caracas. Maybe then we will start all over again—with bicycles."

And I say to him: "That isn't why you do not go into the city, is it? Is it true that you will not go downtown?"

He says: "Yes. Once, when the Congress was nationalizing the oil industry, the President of the Congress came to me and said they wanted me to speak to them. I said, time after time I have been telling you my thinking. So what more can I say? But, the President of the Congress said that I had to come. It was an honor. And I said: In that case you have to use your powers to have the Congress come here. So, they came here, into my garden. The Congress came, to see me."

Don Juan Pablo always, before all else, takes his guests on a tour of his garden. To him, that is the most important thing. He is proudest of the flowers and trees which he has grown in his gardens, his personal Noah's Ark on the edge of the city, his oasis in the world he feels is lost. And as he walks among his plants, he calls each by name. It doesn't matter if his guests are the entire Congress of Venezuela, or a wandering writer from the northern continent.

"See this," he says, fondly touching the petals of a flowering tree. "It is so very delicate, so very fragile, and so very, very lovely."

The loveliest of his trees is perhaps the *El Araguaney,* the national tree of Venezuela, aglow with its bright crown of golden yellow flowers, a majestic tree. One of the tallest in the forest, it towers above all the others. Its wood is so hard and strong that a single cubic foot may weigh sixty to eighty pounds. And, it is the bulwark of the country, used for the building of bridges, docks, railroad ties, fishing rods, boats, canes, and fetishes. But, mostly, he says, it is known for the beauty of its flowers. Near it is the spectacular Rose of Venezuela, a Brownee tree, with its sunbursts of flowers of the deepest red, aflame like burning stars. And beside it, there is the no less dramatic *Arbol del Fuego,* the Tree of Fire, known as the Poinciana, resplendent with the most violent flowers in the forest, as red as fresh blood.

Of his flowers there is no end: the modest *Alocasia,* its pure white cup cradling a perfect stamen, like the vulva of a virgin; the startled oranges of the cockscombs of the Bird of Paradise blossom; the gregarious and joyous *Bougainvillea,* with its swarms of purplish red flowers; the delicate *Amaryllis,* so fragile and so lacelike; the tendrils of the blood red Claw of the Lobster flowers, the *Heliconia;* and the somewhat ominous Dragon's Blood.

Flowers in these tropical forests are not floral decorations. They are larger than life. They are more than human, and they are more sensual than humans ever can be.

In his gorgeous gardens the diminutive don Juan Pablo

is much like a small and happy bird. Beneath the spreading leaves of the palm trees and amidst the bouquets of tropical flowers he seems almost lost from sight, not unwillingly, for this is the world of nature he has come to prefer to the world of petroleum and power.

"Now I am not interested in oil," says don Juan Pablo, the founder of OPEC. "I live for my flowers."

The Production of Paradise

On platforms high above the earth the native people buried their dead. To them death was not solemn but a sacred act of life, as creative as birth. It was not worshipped as those who feared death have thought, but was revered as a renewal of life. So, the dead were placed on a platform beyond the reach of the living, not as a sacrifice, but as an offering to the gods of the sun and sky.

The gods were given these gifts of the dead so that the living might live. And life might go on.

And when you drive north from the ancient city of Coro, through the sands of the deserts of Paraguaná, toward the oil refineries of Cardón, one of these burial platforms may be seen from the highway. It rests on stilts, rising above the sand, as it did in the days when death was still sacred.

On this burial platform there is a carcass of a dead car.

* * *

"If I could determine things, then I would say: I hope that we do not find another drop of oil."

Leonard Withew, Chief of Production
Maraven Refinery, Cardón, Venezuela

* * *

The sand dunes move slowly along the road. In the unending force of the winds from the sea the shifting sand is continually changing the contours of the dunes, but the more they change the more they are the same. Some of the dunes on the road to the oil refinery of Cardón, on the Paraguaná Peninsula, resemble the Sahara; the tourist posters depict them as romantic places where the visitor may ride off on a camel, in the sensuous heat, to erotic rendezvous with the dark-skinned women of the dunes.

But, I see only sand.

Sand penetrates my skin, my mouth, my nostrils, my ears, my eyelids. My body closes all its orifices. And still the sand is in my teeth.

In the dunes there are people who live where no animals can survive. They have been breathing the sand, from childhood, as little fish do water; it is their natural environment, for they know of no other. So, in houses of mud and stone, behind walls of cactuses that attempt, without success, to keep out the winds of sand, they live what seems to outsiders to be desolate lives; and they have children by the year. These children are thin and boney as desert goats. And as naked. For there are no jobs in these deserts, no way to earn money to buy any clothes or shoes.

On the dunes the sands are never silent, never still. The deserts of Paraguaná are surrounded almost entirely by the Caribbean Sea. And so the wind from the sea never seems to cease; like the ferocious sun it scorches the skins of both the people and the earth. People say: "When the wind blows it is terrible. But, when the wind does not blow it is worse."

Even so, in spite of the sea wind and the sea itself, these people of the dunes have hardly any water. The water in the desert is salty and brackish; it is not even good for irrigation. And so pipes bring water from the mainland to this island of sand on the edge of the sea. But, the poor people of the dunes suffer an even stranger irony. Though they live in parched poverty they do so beside some of the largest and richest oil refineries in the world.

On the coast the chimneys of the refinery of Cardón rise like spineless cactuses. In Spanish *cardón* is the word for cactus. But, the refinery is actually a world of fantasy, a place of exotic and magical machinery, its valves and gauges and tanks and pipes glistening in the sun of the desert, a combination of a technological Disneyland and the set of *Star Wars*.

It is an oasis. Surrounding the refinery is a suburban city that is one of the hundreds of by-products of petroleum production with gardens of beautiful tropical flowers and shady trees, modern homes and country clubs, playing fields and cocktail lounges. The community has its own schools, its own stores, its own power plant, its own public services; it is an air-conditioned world unto itself. And if the people of the dunes come here at all it is most likely to work as gardeners and servants.

When the refinery had been owned by Royal Dutch

Shell, armed guards stood at its gates and tightly sealed off the entire community. The gates and guards are now gone, but the barriers still exist that separate the technicians and engineers from the people beyond. One of the new subdivisions of homes now being built is fenced by a high wall which is topped with barbed wire and floodlights, a necessary irony for the nationalized oil industry.

In his offices, on the shores of Lake Maracaibo not far down the coast, the director of the Maraven oil fields, Dr. Nelson Vásquez, ruefully comments on the irony: "Of our country's wealth, two thirds, at least, comes from these oil fields, and three quarters comes from the oil industry. This wealth is now spread throughout the country. And yet, you can walk just five miles from my office, and you won't see any sign of this wealth. It is an anomaly. To the poor people who live outside our compounds we might as well be men from Mars," he says.

Of the not quite fifteen million people in the country no more than twenty-five thousand work in the entire oil industry. There is no need for more. It is an industry of specialists where the small and select group of engineers and technicians produce all the profits from petroleum that the rest of the country lives on—an estimated eleven billion dollars or more a year, every year. In the new industries of advanced technology a developing country no longer needs vast armies of industrial workers when twenty-five thousand men can create profits of eleven billion dollars.

In the fishing villages upon the peninsula it doesn't matter if the men behind the barbed wire of the refinery are foreigners or not. "They are foreigners, to them, even if they are not foreigners," a local official tells me. "In some ways they are considered gods."

Says the Production Chief of the refinery, Leonard

Withew, who coming from Maracaibo is bluntly outspoken: "As you know, Venezuela lives on a bubble of oil which is completely artificial. If that bubble bursts the whole country will go down the drain. We are developing into a country where people are getting used to having money without really having to earn it."

For the rural population in the *campos* and in the new cities the cornucopia of petroleum wealth is more than a mystery; it is magical. It is the new religion.

And in the office of the Director of the refinery, Gustavo Coronel, the exuberant enthusiast of the beneficial wonders of oil production, who is director of the National Petroleum Board as well, the fantastic aspects of the situation remind him of the science fiction stories he reads for relaxation. Coronel laughs: "Every day we generate ninety to one hundred million bolívars. And every day we give it to the country. And we say: 'Here is your daily check!'

"Of course, the country thinks we are magicians," he says. The oil man is the Dr. Faustus of Venezuela; he is both "feared and admired"; he is the sorcerer who magically creates billions of dollars out of a mess of scummy and dirty and ugly black mud. Surely a miracle.

Nor is his technological sleight of hand demystified by the nationalization of the refineries and oil fields by the government, for since then the petroleum profits have "increased tremendously," Dr. Vásquez says. He recalls that John D. Rockefeller once said: "You know, there are two kinds of oil companies—those that are well run and those that are badly run. And both make money." And so, no matter what the oil men do they are fated to become national heroes.

Most of these men have worked in the refineries and oil fields for much of their lives. They held the same jobs with those international oil companies, Shell and Standard Oil, before they were nationalized. So the change from multinational to national ownership was relatively easy. The companies had trained their men expertly. Not merely did the Venezuelan technicians manage the refineries and oil fields, they held high positions in the companies. One was director of the entire Royal Dutch Shell empire from the Caribbean Sea to Argentina. And Coronel, Vasquez, and Withew all had been officials of Shell. So, too, most of the executives of the "socialized" oil industry had been executives of the "imperialistic" multinationals.

"I am a Shell product," the Production Chief, Withew, says frankly. "I cannot deny I have been taught by Shell. I think like a Shell man."

It was easier to change hats than to change minds. There were certain problems of social schizophrenia. "For us it was difficult to realize that from now on Shell was not the parent and we the children," says Withew. "And it was difficult for Shell to understand that they were no longer the owners, but the service contractors.

"Once you become a national company, then your outlook has to change," he says, "because then you no longer first look for corporate profits, but at maximizing the nation's income. Even if it is at the expense of the corporation. That meant undoing a mental condition which had gone on for a hell of a long time. That took us some time. I do not want to use the word shock," he says, "but. . . . "

Even the machinery in the refineries suffered from a bit of schizophrenia though its illness was more technological than pyschological. For years, sensing that nationalization was coming, the companies made no investments or improvements in the plants. They ordered an "absolute minimum of maintenance to keep the refinery going," Withew remembers, "and increasing the capacity of the plants was unheard of.

"Now, the government has gone from austerity to expansion," he says. Everything is changing, is growing, is entirely different, though no one seems quite sure where they are going. It makes the Production Chief uneasy.

For the ebullient Gustavo Coronel this is the great challenge. "The excitement in Venezuela comes from our being a developing country. It is an exciting time to live. When I look at your more technologically advanced country, I feel the excitement is not really there anymore. The excitement we feel is that of the pioneer.

"No, we will not be like children in the technological fields any longer," he says. "We will be equals."

The search for technological independence, to Coronel, is the search for national identity. "We are discovering our own way of doing things. But, the main asset of technological independence is psychological; it makes you feel equal to everyone else," he says. "Nowadays what people admire the most is technology. And so, if we want to be respected and want to respect ourselves, then we have to become proficient in technology. But, I hope, once we are then we will no longer strive for more technology. Because it is not technology that we really wanted, but self-confidence."

It is their love of freedom that will make it possible for Venezuelans to create technology and then reject it, Coronel says. "Freedom is the essential ingredient in our character. It is what makes us unique in South America. This desire for freedom is in our hearts and minds. Well, perhaps not in our hearts, because the heart is helpless, but in our minds."

Many things have uniquely shaped his country's need for freedom, Coronel feels—the heritage of Bolívar and the historical tradition of "getting involved in fighting for liberty all over the world"; the inheritance of stubborn and strong traits from the Venezuelan Indians, "who were very dynamic people"; the "geographic element" of the long coasts that "make us look outward and give us an unconscious sense of universality"; the "obsession we have of always fighting for the underdog and against the world powers through the centuries." And, strangest of all, the influence of the Sephardic Jews!

"Some of our character comes from our racial mixture," says Coronel. "There were Indians who mixed with the Spanish, many of whom were Jewish, Spanish Jews, who converted to Catholicism and who were fleeing from Spain. Many of these Jews made their way to Venezuela. There are a tremendous number of prominent families in Venezuela who are no longer Jewish, but who have Jewish roots." Some of the oldest families still bear Sephardic names; the name Pérez is one.

And in Coro, one of the first cities built by the *conquistadors*, there is a sixteenth-century *Cemeterio Hebreo,* the most ancient cemetery in the country. "You have never heard of our Jewish *conquistadors*?" Coronel laughs. "Ah, but it is the truth. These Jewish elements have contributed to our hunger for freedom, I think."

In that heritage Coronel sees some of the sources of the quickness and restlessness by which Venezuelans are so often characterized. He feels it is the clue to the way his countrymen and women are beginning to master modern technology.

"Maybe your country took two hundred years to do what we are trying to do in twenty," he says. "That is not because we want to, but because we have to. I do not say it is a good way to develop. But, it is the only way. We have no time. And we feel obliged to live as well as you do, and to be as strong as you. At whatever price." Romantic as he is, the Director is not blind to the dangers of technological success. "Always you have to pay the price for getting where you want to go. That price is always too high," he says. "And when you get there you realize that it isn't what you really want."

Nonetheless, the allure of technology will seduce the Third World, Coronel says. "And what is happening here is going to happen in all of the undeveloped countries."

Dr. Vasquez is not convinced. He scoffs at those, like the "religious fanatics of progress," who believe in the inevitability of industrialism. In his office, beneath a Van Gogh print, he leans back from his desk, with its novels by Hermann Hesse, and motions to his bookcases where the books of Mao Tse-tung lie beside technological tomes on petroleum drilling.

"My God, if anyone would read the history of the world they would know it is a mistake," he says. "By now we should have learned. These massive projects of development, I don't think they lead to development, I don't think they lead to development at all. When we spend billions for a huge petrochemical complex, which I was asked to direct, and create jobs for three thousand people, that's absurd. It would be much better to invest in farms, so our people could eat."

"Every developing country is making the same mistake, at this very moment. The beautiful theory is, 'Let's industrialize now! We are coming to the takeoff period in our economy!' And this theory is independent of political viewpoints. Socialist or capitalist, it is all quite the same. The Russians made the same mistakes under Stalin, with all his beautiful plans. He was quite mad. Not in the sense of power, but in the sense of a plan to create 'happiness' for the people by engineering their souls. And we do it too. No one is daring enough to take a different route. One of our historians has written that the generation of Bolivar was a generation of geniuses, but it begat generations of idiots.

"Maybe we are not building great cities, but are building great ruins," Dr. Vásquez says.

And if Dr. Vásquez is critical of the country's development, Leonard Withew is despairing. The precise and puritanical chemical engineer, by his own description, is as unforgiving as a confessional priest listening to his own recitation of his sins.

"Sometimes I see ourselves, the oil people, as custodians of a perishable asset that will not last too long," he says. "Perhaps twenty years. The time is running out. For forty years we have been saying this. Now we are in a worse position than we were in 1940. Now we depend even more on oil. And this is our real challenge. I don't see our challenge in maintaining the supply of oil, or the oil industry. Production of oil is not a question of technology; it is a question of morality," Withew says. "We are not even feeding ourselves. We don't produce enough food. Let's start with that. Let's start preparing ourselves to live in the real world. We have to take a good, hard look at ourselves, at what we are doing. We have to build a more realistic society. I would like to see Venezuela face itself.

"Though I know that any new discovery of oil is good for the nation, and it means the standard of living rises and we get more money, if I could determine things then I would say that I hope we do not find another drop of oil. Let's forget about oil!" says the Production Chief.

Men like these seem more like philosophers, or clergymen, than the executives of the oil industry. The stereotype of the oil man does not fit. Perhaps there is a defensiveness in their *mea culpas,* but as Coronel says, these are men "who look out of a very wide window." They have been educated in Europe and America. And they have lived and worked all over the world, from Australia to Indonesia to England.

Coronel, elated that the discussion has avoided the usual statistics of petroleum production and has concerned itself instead with the state of the Venezuelan soul, becomes even more effusive than he normally is. He exclaims: "It is good to talk of philosophical things. The man who has no philosophy of life is not Venezuelan. In our country many of the technical people are a little ashamed of being technicians. For a Venezuelan, up to now, everyone's secret ambition was to be a philosopher or a poet. And we like to think that technology is a necessary evil; it is not what a man should search for. In a world where technology is god, we just want to dominate enough of it so we can be rid of our inferiority complex. But, in our hearts we do not want to be a technological power. Secretly we just want to be philosophers and poets.

"In the refinery you may see technicians wearing their safety helmets, but in their back pockets they may have books of poems," he says a little shyly, as if he is describing himself.

To illustrate his words, Coronel annouces: "Let me show you one of my favorite cultural pursuits. I am trying to make the refinery as beautiful as a painting. For me it is not enough that the refinery is efficient; it must be 'a thing of beauty.' And so I am painting the whole refinery in all the colors of the rainbow."

"Are you joking?" I ask.

"No, I will show you," he says. And there it is.

Some of the pipes have been painted deep purple. Some of the pipes are a luminous gold. Some of the tanks are Prussian blue. Some of the distillation vats are shocking pink. It is a fantasy, but the fantasy is real.

"Is it not beautiful?" Coronel asks. "You see, even machinery can be given our Venezuelan face."

To beautify the refinery even more, they have begun to

plant trees in the desert. In the evenings the men, led by Coronel, go out along the barren roads that lead across the windswept dunes and amid the blowing sands and gaunt cactuses, and try to plant rows of trees.

"Come back in two years and I will show you how the trees have grown," he says. "You see, some have taken root."

It is true. Not all the trees have died at once. Some are stubbornly holding on to their leaves. But at least half have been stripped bare by the wind and the sun and the fates. Even the best magician with every trick cannot produce the illusion of paradise.

The wind comes up. It is dry and it is hot, gathering up the sensual heat and rancid odors of the desert. On these dunes the sand begins to insidiously sift through the darkness, covering up the evidence of the people and the animals which had been left during the day. No one leaves a footprint in the desert.

And the long talks of the day seem to linger and fade with the blowing of the wind. But the night is empty and the talk is stilled.

In the lounge of the La Casona bar and restaurant the lights go on. Not that it matters. The lights are red bulbs that shine as darkly by day as by night. And no one in the bar can see anyone else, which is fine, since men have come here so they may be unseen. Some of the men from the refinery come here just for that. In the desert sun there is no privacy; it is like being naked.

The lonely men sit in the red-lit darkness and peer with red-lit eyes into the darkness. For love. But there are no women, there is no one in the bar but the engineers and technicians from the refinery who have come here so often they are tired of the sight of one another. Only one of them is drunk enough to have forgotten he is not alone.

In the evening there is an occasional bad movie in town. And in the town nearby there are bad movies every night. Besides that, there is television and the usual sports and social clubs. There is drinking. "Culturally and spiritually we are a whiskey-drinking country," Coronel has said to me; but the men who come to the La Casona do not come to drink; they come for the comforting darkness of the red lights.

On the wall of his office, behind his desk where most visitors cannot see it, Dr. Vásquez has a print of the Bosch painting, "The Garden of Earthly Delights," with its hundreds of naked men and women caressing in every possible, and impossible, position of pleasure and pain. The landscape of love is a paradise of fantasies, as lonely as it is crowded, as ecstatic as it is pathetic, as mocking as it is erotic.

"Now, why do you have this here?" I ask Dr. Vásquez.

"That," he laughs, "is the portrait of the workers in my oil company. And of every company in the oil industry.

So the men of the refinery in the bleak deserts of the Paraguaná Peninsula come and sit and drink and wait in the dark red light for a glimpse of "The Garden of Earthly Delights." But, no one can see in the darkness.

On the wall of the air-conditioned lounge of the La Casona there is a photographic mural of the Rocky Mountains. It covers an entire wall. The forests upon the mountainsides are thick with snow and the lake is frozen. Anyone who opens the door of the lounge lets the sand from the dunes blow onto the snowy mountains.

It is still early in the evening. But the men begin to leave. In the morning the workday in the refinery will begin at dawn and these men have to be at work on time; the production of paradise depends on their efficiency; and the faith of the country, in its future, depends on their fantasies.

The sand in the streets blows in from the dunes. It never ceases.

* * *

On the shores of a quiet lagoon there is an abandoned bamboo hut. The lagoon is so serene not even the birds ruffle its waters. It is a deep pool, so deep that its surface looks black. That may be because the lagoon, hidden in the depths of the forest and terraced with flowering vines and lush tropical fruits, is covered with a thickened black scum of crude oil that oozes from a nearby oil well.

There is a dead coral snake in the lagoon. It cannot sink.

Sitting on the Delta of the Orinoco and Thinking of Progress

On the delta of the Orinoco River the earth dissolves into the sea. It is that hot and humid. So hot that the dense growth of the tropical forest bathes my skin with a second skin of sweat. The ferns and bushes engulf everything like tepid waves of water. There is no escape from the heat and the humidity. And when you come here you soon learn to wear your skin of sweat as casually as you can, for there is no other way. Those who try to struggle against the jungle succumb to it.

So when the heat has entangled my mind like a maze of vines, I no longer resist it. The forest seems oppressive and impenetrable when you fight it. And yet, in time, even I may learn to surrender to its overwhelming heat. Then even I shall become as peaceful as the Indian sitting beneath a eucalyptus tree with his flute-like poison dart blower lying gently in between his knees.

To live in a tropical forest one has to be at peace with the environment; hostility is impractical.

* * *

On the radio a Calypso singer on the island of Trinidad off the coast of the Orinoco Delta is singing in a raucous and erotic voice:

> Maybe your front is fine,
> But when I catch you
> Your behind will be mine.

No one can make love in the tropical heat, it seems to me, unless they can do it without moving too much. It's just too hot.

Someone has evidently learned the way it's done. The villages in the jungle are full of naked children.

* * *

The man sits on his wooden chair in the dirt courtyard of his bamboo hut. He places his chair in exactly the same place every day. There he sits all day, every day—in the morning, in the afternoon, in the evening. It seems as if he is doing nothing but sitting. But he is working. He is watching the earth move, the sun rise and fall, the fruits ripen, the shapes of the leaves change, the poisonous snakes come and go. And these things will determine how well his family will live, or die.

In the courtyard of his bamboo hut the whole world revolves around the man who sits there. He need not go in search of it; it comes to him. That means he is the center of his world and not that the world is the center of him. So he need merely sit where he is. And keep his eyes open.

The eyes and senses of these people who live in the forests are the tools of their technology. And theirs is a precise and economical scientific method of studying the world around them, that uses only renewable and non-consumptive energy, the energy of their bodies, for they cannot use what they do not have. Lord Keynes would be as lost in the jungle as some tourist with a credit card.

And so the scholars of the forests sit and silently watch. Their schools are wherever they sit. Their technology is in themselves. That comprehension is evident in their grace.

On the delta of the Orinoco there are people who seem expert when it comes to sitting. Some do so with such mastery that the most difficult postures of their repose, resembling an Amazonian yogi, seem effortless and almost casual. It is as if by feigning boredom they are attempting to conceal the intellectual activity of their bodily senses, for when the flesh thinks there is always the danger of evoking the wrath of the gods. So it may be wiser for the body to pretend ignorance of the mind.

It is a subtle art. From an early age boys and girls have to be taught the skill of sitting still. No wonder the villagers are amazed to meet people from the cities who do not seem to know how to sit still at all. Why are you always in such a hurry, they ask? Why are you rushing about? How will you ever learn anything?

And so I try to sit as still as they do. But I cannot. I am not naked. Sitting in a tropical forest is not natural when the body is clothed with layers of nylon and plastic and polyester. The clothing that I am wearing dulls the sensitivity of my skin to the world around me. And so sitting becomes boring; the clothing that I wear is designed to protect and defend my body against the urban world where it is manufactured, so it cannot be injured by the city. For if the body is naked then it is opened to the sensations around it and it feels the most subtle things. And the senses of the skin are added to the five senses of the head. That, in the city, may be dangerous.

The men, women, and children in the villages along the Orinoco do not suffer from that fear. For they are wholly naked to their world.

Sitting is not as easy as it may seem to be. It is a skill, a profession, a devotion, a science for studying life, that requires a lifetime to learn. While to the uninitiated sitting may appear to be the lethargic occupation of lazy men, it is as tiring to sit still, for hours, as it is to walk for hours. In some ways it may be more strenuous.

Sitting on the earth is as different from sitting on the grass as sitting under a tree is from sitting on the edge of the road, sitting against a wall from sitting on one's heels, sitting in a hammock from sitting in a chair, sitting in the sun from sitting in the shade, sitting as a young girl does from the way an old man may sit. There are as many individual ways of sitting as there are individual ways of contemplating life. And the slightest change in posture will alter one's perception.

One morning I see a man come from his bamboo hut and sit on his chair. He looks dissatisfied. The chair, it seems, is in a poor position, for his vision of his world is incomplete. So he rises and he carefully moves the chair and tentatively sits down again, looks about, squinting to scrutinize his domain, rises once more and once more moves his chair until he finds the proper position from which he can see his entire world.

In the afternoon when I go by his hut he is still sitting

there. The earth has moved, and so has he, though he has not moved at all.

* * *

The sun burns the surface of the water; it is a white fire that ignites the river and the flames scorch the entire town.

No one is on the streets. After the noonday meal the delta town of Tucupita goes to sleep. One by one shopkeepers put the shutters on their stores and lock their doors and go home. In the empty plaza a policeman wanders aimlessly about with nothing to do and no one to talk to. And in the fetid hotel above the dry goods store the young Indian whores are asleep.

But I cannot sleep. I rise from the moist sheets of the hotel bed, take a cold shower that I share with a cockroach who scurries away in displeasure, and don my English safari jacket, a remnant of bygone colonialism, to go out into the noonday sun.

On the river the huge dugout canoes of the Waraos float at bay. No one is on the river at midday. The old men sit along the bank, in the shade, waiting for the evening breeze. In the meantime the canoes idle on the water's edge like great beached fish. Their hulls are hollowed from the trunks of majestic trees, six to seven feet across and thirty to forty feet long, for in the days before the coming of the Europeans these were seagoing canoes used in trade and travel from island to island in the Caribbean. Storytellers still tell of the exploits of those voyages in legends which some call folklore.

Now the seafarers of the Waraos do not go far to sea. They wait for the evenings when the tourists and the anthropologists will go sightseeing, to see the Warao carving their canoes.

In the plaza three young Indian boys are looking at a movie poster. The *Cine Orinoco,* beside the Catholic church, is playing *La Esposa Virgen*, *The Married Virgin*, starring Carroll Baker. But the show will not begin until evening, for the theater is steaming and has no air-conditioning. The boys are not, however, interested in the white virgin and they eye the poster of the coming attraction on which a naked Indian, waving a rifle, is yelling his defiance at General Custer in a movie whose title has been lost in translation.

The boys are fascinated. One of them points excitedly to the rifle. The Waraos of the Orinoco Delta, whose villages they have come from, have few guns. Some speak of the Waraos as the "peaceful people" much as the tribes further up river are always described as being "fiercely warlike," though that is the distinction made by non-Indians. On the Orinoco the people simply call themselves the People; they smile at the judgments of the strangers and say nothing, a silence that is seen as their acquiescence, when it is merely caution.

On the riverbanks the dense growth of bushes and vines make it difficult to see more than a few feet. Everything is muted. The sounds and sights of the forest seem to come from the distance, even when they are underfoot. In these natural places the people have to live as part of nature, with an intimacy and openness that city dwellers always see as violent and primitive. But, violence in the forest is much less frequent than in the city. And that may be because it is more direct and deadly.

When the Waraos come to the city they become subdued. The noise and traffic and talking do violence to them and they become fearful. So they may try to withdraw from the evil of the city, much as city people do from what they see as the evil of the forest.

And yet, in the town of Tucupita the forest people look much the same as the city people. That may be because so many of the townspeople are partly Indian; an inheritance that may be hidden by their blue jeans and sport shirts, but is visible in their eyes and the poise with which they walk to hide their unease. The city seems uncivilized to them, and they try to become as inconspicuous as they possibly can.

Still, they come to Tucupita because it is the biggest town in the Orinoco Delta. It is, as well, the office of the Regional Director of the Central Office for Indigenous Affairs. He is a governmental missionary sent from the capital to preserve the tribes and he administers the governmental funds which the tribes receive.

In the tropical heat, it seems to me that the one man who might be at his desk when everyone else is asleep, might be the Regional Director for Indigenous Affairs. He is in his office, sitting at his desk, by himself.

Señor Edith Arzoby is "in charge" of all the forest people in the Orinoco Delta, a region that is three hundred kilometers wide and one hundred kilometers deep, reaching to the borders of Guayana. There are at least two hundred and fifty tribal groups in these forests. And it is his missionary task to protect all of them from contemporary society. He is a modern missionary, not of the old religions, but of the new sociology. In fact, he is a sociologist.

And he is a black man. In an office that is modest and unpretentious, he sits alone with that genial, but solemn countenance of the contemporary colonial servant entrusted with a too great responsibility, whose diffident manner is reminiscent of a Graham Greene hero, devoted and doomed, if such a hero were black, not white. The office is orderly and its piles of official papers are all neatly stacked in their proper places—and so is Señor Arzoby.

In a self-conscious way he seems uneasy at being a black man "in charge" of red men. So he tells me more belligerently than is necessary: "One the people in these offices were almost all Indians. Some were *caciques,* you know, chiefs. They made speeches about helping their people, but they were always fighting each other for the government money. And they took the money to buy cars and houses for their personal benefit. They took the foods and medicines the government gave them for their people. And they sold them. They were not real Indians. They were capitalistic Indians," he says disapprovingly. "They were uneducated. Some day an Indian will be sitting at my desk again. But he will have to be educated. He will have to be a 'civilized' Indian.

"Many of these forest people still live as they were," he says, "before the Europeans came. Many of them are isolated from civilization and hard to reach. Even today, many of them have not been reached by civilization. In the region of Antonio Díaz most of the people are as they were. They are very primitive."

And I ask him: "How do these 'uncivilized' people live in a Third World country rich with the black gold of OPEC?"

"In the past they lived by gathering fruits, and by fishing," he says. "Now the river is polluted by the garbage and industrial waste of the factories. And so the fish give them diseases. And now we are teaching them to grow rice, with modern machines, and not eat fish. Of course they still gather fruits."

And I ask him: "How many of these 'uncivilized' people are there?"

"No one knows exactly," he answers. "There may be fifteen thousand living in the labyrinth of pools and lagoons deep in the swamps of the Orinoco." Since his office seems to count as Indians merely those who "live as they were," the figures may be too small. Once the forest people come into the towns and begin to wear blue jeans and get jobs and become parents of urban children they no longer are thought of as Indians. It is as if the racial codes of the Spanish empire still existed.

"Civilized" and "uncivilized." If these definitions of an Indian were used, not more than one tenth of the people who were considered to be Indians in the United States would be counted as such. So, conversely, there may be ten times as many Indians as the quarter of a million that are recognized in Venezuela; they may be one quarter of the nation.

And I ask him: "Why are you trying to preserve these 'uncivilized' people?"

"The colonists from Spain exploited the Indians as slaves," he says. "No one can now go into Indian territory without permission from the government. We protect them. We have programs to teach them to read and write their own languages. And, we wish to preserve their culture."

Behind his desk, on the wall, is a map of the Orinoco. I get up and with my finger point to the most remote villages of the Warao. And I ask him: "Suppose petroleum and iron were discovered here where the Warao live, would you protect them? What would happen to them?"

"They would have to move," he says. "But we would protect them. It would be like what has happened where the government is building the Guri dam, the largest dam in America. There were indigenous people living there and the government moved them to a better place."

And I ask him: "Suppose they say, 'This is our land! We will not move!' "

"No, they cannot stand in the way of progress," he says. "If they protest it will do no good. The government will say our natural resources are for the benefit of the whole nation and no one can stand in the way."

And I ask him: "Suppose they say these natural resources are on their land, so they belong to them. Isn't there a law in Venezuela that says that the government 'guarantees and recognizes the rights of indigenous populations . . . to hold the lands, woods, and waterways which they occupy or which belong to them . . . without detriment of their incorporation to the national society?' That is the law, isn't it? So, just as Venezuela organized OPEC to protect its natural resources from exploitation, suppose the Indians join OPEC to protect their natural resources from exploitation—by Venezuela?"

"No, that is not possible!" he says. The thought agitates him. And he pounds his desk. "They cannot do that! No, no, no! If they said that, the government would say: 'Even if your land is Indian land it is Venezuelan. And even if you may be Indian, you are Venezuelans. You must obey the nation.' And you must not forget that most of our Indians are 'uncivilized,' " he says. "They are not educated enough to think in these ways.

"Come with me," the Regional Director says, "and I will show you the 'real' Indians." In a few days he will leave upon a journey to the remote tribes. By boat he will go to the isolated villages of the Warao, to bring them foods and medicines, a trip that takes five days, and he invites me to come with him so that I can see what the government is trying to do for these "uncivilized" people.

"You cannot see 'real' Indians in the cities," he says.

On the ceiling a fan turns in redundant rhythm. It moves the heat about the room from one place to another, like the leaves of a palm tree swaying unendingly, but going nowhere. In the empty streets of the town there is a slight stirring. The evening breeze lifts the dust on the plaza and blows it across the street. Some of the old Warao men sitting on the riverbanks look up, see that nothing is happening, and close their eyes again. In the old hotel the young Indian whores are begining to awaken. The lights go on in the plaza and they give the town a carnival look. But, there is no carnival.

On the trails through the forest the young Warao have begun to walk toward the town. Some are wearing shoes. Some are barefoot. As the sun goes down, under the shadows of the trees, they walk slowly, for they know there will not be much happening in the town when they get there. Those who have a few cents in the pockets of their blue jeans may buy a ticket to the movie and see *La Esposa Virgen*, or buy a beer. Mostly, the merchants of Tucupita have nothing to sell to the poor Indians but the clothes of poverty.

Still, it is said that in the Orinoco basin, under their feet, where these boys and girls walk there may be the largest deposits of oil tar in all the world. There are said to be half a billion tons of bauxite, to make aluminum. There are entire mountains of iron. And the wealth of these things is so great the diamonds and gold are insignificant.

On the bare earth the bare feet of the Warao boys and girls tread lightly. They make no sound. They say nothing at all, to anyone.

* * *

In the deep forest, in a clearing, the government has benevolently built a row of modern houses for the Warao people. They are sturdy houses, constructed of cement blocks, with real doors and windows that can lock. In these symbols of urban life, set in the tropical jungles, the rooms have been plastered and whitewashed as neatly as those in any suburban subdivision. These houses are meant to be a learning experience, in which the forest people will teach themselves how to live in the city.

But the people of the forest will not live in the houses. In the clearing behind the cement buildings are several huge brush shelters. Roofed not by palm leaves, but with tin bought in the town, the traditional structures house entire families. In the open air, for the brush shelters have no walls, the people have hung their hammocks for sleeping, and on the dirt floors have spread their mats for sitting, and in the open fires have set their clay pots for cooking. And so they go on living as they always have. No one stays inside the cement houses. In the heat they become ovens. However, the government houses are not entirely empty and abandoned.

In the cement buildings the Warao keep their pigs.

The Guájito: The Tribes of Little Venice

Four women walk along the beach in flowery flowing robes, barefoot on the sand, like fanciful and flamboyant Bedouins of the tropics, their billowing gowns blowing in the evening wind from the sea. They are the women of the *Guájito* Indians. And they walk with the dignity of princesses in front of their bamboo and mud huts, a phalanx of beautiful and majestic women. If they are not the most beautiful women on earth, they are surely the most stately.

And that is how they walk in the evening—with a dignity that no one can see but themselves. They are as straight as the mangrove trees that line the nearby lagoons.

One wears a red robe with golden flowers, one an orange robe with greenish flowers, one a white robe with pink flowers, one a purple robe with blue flowers. These robes clothe them from neck to ankle, in swirling circles of cloth.

In the plaza of their village the *Guájito* women stand together as if posed. They form ensembles. And they resemble the Greek choruses of mythic dramas, oracles of Armageddon, silently awaiting a second coming of Aphrodite, or the arrival of Moses—on the bus from Maracaibo, bearing the Eleventh Commandment.

These women seem to stay together. Few men are among them, for unless they walk with their husbands, they walk only with other women.

In the evening the *Guájito* women come by the hundreds to stand along the highway. They seem to be waiting for the evening wind. When it comes in from the sea, swaying the leaves of the palm trees, they too sway. But if their dresses are like palm leaves, their torsos are like the trunks of the trees. These women do not give ground to the wind, but confront it, face-to-face, with a certain disdain, and peace. Sometimes they will sit along the highway, with their backs to the pavement. It too is a posture of disdain, for like their sisters these women may be waiting for a ride, but they will not ask for it. Instead, they sit in silence, letting the wind toss their hair as it tosses their gowns, enjoying their defiance.

And still the women come to the highway by the hundreds and hundreds. It is an awesome sight. The whole world of the *Guájito* seems to be a world of women. But of course that cannot be.

Seldom do the *Guájito* women wear anything underneath their robes. And so the wind caresses them with a thousand fingers. In the evening the wind is cool and soothing on their humid skin. Their faces are serene.

One woman, older than the rest, is standing all alone. She is screaming in the wind. Her face is as distorted as a face of a *bruja,* for she is either a witch, or she is mad.

So none of the other women go near the old woman. If

she is cursing their existence as women, as the pain of being a woman screams from her mouth, so they are guarding their existence as women, and the joy of being a woman. But they seem to be guarding more than themselves. They have the appearance of soldiers standing guard before their huts and around their villages. It is as if these *Guájito* women come out at night to protect their children and their men.

At the University of Maracaibo, an anthropologist explains: "The *Guájito* are a matriarchal society. Not only are the family names and lands inherited through the women, but because of this the women play an important part in ruling the society itself.

"These women are the guardians of the *Guájito* way of life," he says. And he ought to know. This anthropologist is a *Guájito.*

On the hills and on the beaches, and on the highways of the coast of the Caribbean, the women remain on guard until the sun has set in a bloody confrontation with the darkness. And then they go, one by one, into their bamboo and mud huts and draw the darkness in with them like the skirts of their robes.

And then the children and the men of the *Guájito* know night has come.

* * *

On the billboards John Wayne and Clint Eastwood are sulking. A goat, who is oblivious to their piercing eyes and smoking pistols, is contentedly eating the peeling papers of their posters. But the young Indian men who have come to town on this Saturday eye the movie posters in anticipation. After a day of drinking and loving they will soothe their squinting eyes in the cool darkness of the theater and yell encouragement to these heroes of North America as they courageously kill Indians.

El Moján is the most popular town in the *Guájito* country. It has a movie theater.

On the weekends the young Indian men come into the provincial town from miles around. In the cafes on the corner of the dusty plaza they sit drinking beer and soda pop, waiting for something to happen. But nothing does. The circus by the sea, with its ferris wheel and rides, is still until evening. So, in the lethargy of the noon heat the young men go to the houses on the side streets, where between the moist sheets and their dreams they imagine they are caressing Marilyn Monroe and Jane Fonda.

The noon hour lasts all afternoon. In time, the young men wander down to the seawall, by the blue lagoon, with its beach of beer cans. On the wall of the latrine someone has painted in bold brushstrokes: YOUNG MEN, THE ARMY IS THE PRISON OF THE POOR! DO NOT GO!

But, where can the young men go? In the *Guájito* country there are but two ways that men may be men, in the old way. One is to become a smuggler of contraband on the beaches and the other is to become a soldier who hunts the smugglers.

On the road that goes from El Moján, into the jungle, there is a Market of Thieves that stretches for at least half a mile. In the bamboo stalls almost everything imaginable is sold: a case of whiskey from Scotland, Yardley soaps from England, large jars of Nescafé from Switzerland, Agua Brava shaving cologne from Spain. And, I am told, at some stalls a young girl or boy may be bought for a very reasonable price.

Night and day huge diesel trucks of unknown origins

with unknown cargoes roll through the town. Somewhere in the jungles they are loaded with the illicit wonders of the world.

"Where do they come from?" I ask.

"Ah, who knows," I am told.

On the beaches along the shores the people once lived in bamboo houses which were built on stilts high above the water. When the *conquistadors* came from Spain and first saw these houses the scene reminded them of the canals of Venice. And so they called the land Little Venice, or Venezuela.

And the people lived on the water because they were ancient seafarers and traders. It was as if their houses rose from the sea, much as the oil wells on Lake Maracaibo now seem to rise from the water. The *Guájito* were known as an adventurous and daring people. In those days the Spaniards feared them so greatly that for centuries they did not disturb their villages by the sea, and as the years went by the houses of the *Guájito* became refuges for the pirates who sailed the Caribbean and the *Guájito* became skilled at piracy.

Now when these young Indians come to El Moján on weekends the most heroic thing they can do is to go to a movie to watch Clint Eastwood and John Wayne kill Indians.

* * *

On the Colombian border where the tangled jungles of far western Venezuela create a barrier impenetrable to all but the *Guájito* Indians, on a serene and hidden lagoon deep in the mangrove swamps, there stands the abandoned house of the *Arawak* people's great *cacique,* who was known as *El Torito,* the Little Bull, who was the son of *El Torito,* the Great One, the legendary chief of the people of the coastal jungles.

The road to his house is now rutted in the sand. Father and son are both dead now.

In a field surrounded by barbed wire a man is farming. He does not answer our calls. He is a country Indian and he does not understand English, or Spanish, for he speaks only *Guájito.* Nonetheless, he seems to understand our request to see the *cacique,* for he smiles. And says nothing.

The man is wearing a straw hat and a red polo shirt. His only other clothing is a loin cloth; it is a flowered polyester that he wears in the traditional way, knotted at his crotch. Red seems to be his favorite color, for his house is painted a bright blood red.

When we are about to get back into the car, he waves to us. And without a word, he comes running, leaping the barbed wire fence, like a young man, and with his hands he tells us he will take us there. The man points down the road. And he gets into our car. Smiling at our surprise, he offers his hand.

Sitting in the front seat of the car, he hunches forward as if ready to jump out at any moment. He says nothing. Once more he indicates the direction with his hand, guiding us until we come to a compound under a grove of palm trees where he gets out, shakes hands, waves, and without a word runs off, trotting back to his farm.

An old man comes out and opens the cattle gate. In a few moments a tall and simply dressed man emerges from the cluster of huts and sheds. Though he could not have known we were coming, he welcomes us casually, as though he were expecting us. He is gracious and polite. Nemesio Montiel is his name, and he is the son-in-law of *El*

Torito; his wife is the eldest daughter of the *cacique.* That makes him a respected and powerful man. For the *Guájito* people inherit not only their family name and land through their women, but their family honor, as well.

Even so he seems a modest man. He is friendly and informal. He has none of the mannerisms of a head of state. A man whose people reign over the beaches and mountains that are as strategic and rich as these might be expected to strut his power. But he does not.

There is no hint of his powers in his gentle smile. Some of the richest oil deposits in the world, worth billions of dollars, lie beneath the lands where the *Guájito* people have lived for centuries, but he says nothing of this oil wealth. One boast is all he makes as he introduces himself. Just one.

"Myself, I have thirty-eight children," he says. "Twelve of them are professionals. Four are in the university right now. Yes, thirty-eight children. That isn't too bad."

Some say he is seventy, but he has the appearance of a much younger man. He is proud of his vigor.

Beneath a mahogany tree he sets up some chairs. He bids us be seated. His son brings a tray with little demitasse cups of coffee. The china cups are painted with yellow flowers. And the son-in-law of the *cacique* says: "Do you take sugar?" So our conversation about the life and the death of his people begins.

And I say: "How are things with the *Guájito*?"

He says: "Now there is a terrible drought. The cattle are dying. The land is too dry to be farmed. We call the rain. But, the rain does not come. We have had the rain ceremonies. But, the rain does not come. We have danced and worn the proper masks and things. But, the rain still does not come."

And I say: "Maybe your prayers have not been good."

He says: "Sometimes everything is wrong. When your scientists call the rain, does it come?"

And I say: "But, the *Guájito* people, they are still strong?"

He says: "There are maybe one, two, or three hundred thousand *Guájitos.* Maybe more. No one knows how many. And we speak many dialects and live in many different places, but we are all *Guájito.*

"We are one nation. Some of us live in Venezuela. Some in Colombia. And some in Panama. But, we are all the same nation. It does not matter what you call us, for we are what we are. You know, the *Guájito* go back and forth over these borders, all the borders. It does not matter to us. You know, we vote in both countries. Because it is all one country. It is our country."

And I say: "In times like this how do the *Guájito* survive?"

He says: "Some people farm. Some people do selling. On the beaches and in the mountains they say there is much contraband. They say there is smuggling. Even whiskey from Scotland that comes to the island in the Caribbean, and from there to here, somewhere. Big ships bring it. That is what they say. And they say there are high government officials involved. I do not say who. That is what they say.

"Then, there is the weed, the weed they call marijuana. Sometimes the government tries to kill it by spraying it from airplanes. Sometimes they raid the fields. But on the Colombia side of the border, I hear, they say there are hundreds of hectares of the weed. Everyone comes for the weeds. The North Americans, the Germans, the Italians, the Greeks. They all love the weeds. You know why? Because the weed is money. And they all love money. So we survive."

And I say: "And what about the oil men who come here?"

He says: "When the oil men came, in the beginning, some of our people did not wish them to come here. So, they shot at them. If I did not go with these oil men they could not have come here."

And I say: "Where?"

He says: "Where you cannot go! In the uncivilized country! Where no one can go but the *Guájito!*"

And I say: "What do you mean by the 'uncivilized country'?"

He says: "Come when the rainy season is ended and I will go there with you. You can go there only in a four-wheel drive. It is where only the *Guájito* can go. That is why we can survive, you see, because there are places, even now, where only we can go. That is why we survive."

And I say: "They say the *Guájito* have no *cacique* now. If you have no *cacique,* how can you survive?"

He says: "The elders have not yet chosen a *cacique* because they say no one is qualified. Not now. Some time, but not now.

"To be a *cacique* one must have the proper qualities. One, he must be a good farmer, he must know the earth. And two, he must be a man of courage, a brave man, who has a brave heart. And three, he must have a knowledge of economics, how capitalism works, so he can help our people profit in the marketplace. And four, he must have an intelligent mind, he has to know what the others think, so he can protect our people against their thinking.

"When *El Torito* was our *cacique,* he could do all these things. He could not read. He could not write. But, he had all of the four qualities. One day, when the dictator, General Jiménez, came here, *El Torito* asked him a question. *El Torito* asked the dictator a question which he could not answer. And, so, we are waiting for a *cacique* who can ask questions they cannot answer. We can wait."

And I say: "These things, these oil men and smugglers and weed lovers, aren't they corrupting the spirit of the *Guájito*? Isn't all this destroying you? Isn't it bad for your people?"

He says: "No. When our young people go to work in the cities, they almost always come home to our people. Even the professionals almost always come home. Once you are a *Guájito,* you know, you are always a *Guájito.* Always! No one can change that. We say everyone who is an Indian is a *Guájito.* They are born a *Guájito.* They die a *Guájito.* So, that is the way it is. No one can change that.

"Now, we have three hundred of our young people who are in the university, who are professionals. Soon these young people will come home, to help us. And we wait for that. When they come home, then the time will come for us to proclaim the *Guájito* nation. Our own nation. Not the nation of others. Our own nation. Maybe then we will have a plebiscite, you know, what you call a democratic vote. We can wait."

The son-in-law of the *cacique* once more smiled his gentle smile. It was all he wished to say.

On the lagoon, under the mahogany tree, deep in the mangrove swamp, beneath the isthmus where the Panama Canal once had been dug through their land, the people waited while all the foreigners argued among themselves about who owned the man-made river of water that flowed from one ocean to the other. No one has asked them who they thought owned the land of their ancestors.

And so, they waited.

The Black Villagers

In the market of Carúpano there are dozens of stalls where all sorts of fish are sold. One black woman is selling small sharks that lie peacefully in the apron of her skirt; another black woman has her stall piled high with piranhas, the vicious teeth that can devour a man in minutes ghoulishly displayed by their open mouths. But, the unusual thing is not the fish. Both of these black women have blue eyes, and nearby there is a black child with a blonde Afro.

Carúpano is on the coast where the ships of Columbus landed. His statue is still standing in the plaza. For centuries the town has been the port of refugees and slaves fleeing from the outside world, as cosmopolitan as can be found in the land, a refuge to which even Papillon, on his escape from Devil's Island, sought in his flight from the moralities of society. Ever since the black men and women of West Africa were brought here as slaves, and abandoned on the remote sands and mountains, the peninsula of Paria has hidden its inhabitants from the rest of Venezuela. No one has bothered them, for there is little to be exploited here but beds of sea salt. And fish.

And so, the children of this town of Carúpano have been borne beyond the institutions and prohibitions of racial judgments. They wear their blonde Afros naturally.

Still, in the fishing villages by the sea the graffiti of the black fishermen comment sardonically on the crossing of the color line. Their dark laughter is vulgar.

On the wall of one hut there is a huge painting of a Chinese dragon that is spitting red fire on a five foot tall egg from which a frightened white chicken has emerged. On the wall of another hut is a larger than life drawing of a white woman who has dropped her panties around her ankles as she bends over to offer her upraised pink rump to every man who passes in the street. On the wall of the third hut there is the painting of an Indian *cacique* with a feathered headdress, and a white cock in his mouth.

The love of brotherhood is often bitter.

* * *

The fishing village of El Morro de Punto Santo straddles a sand bar on the peninsula of Paria. It is a poor village where the people live by selling mussels they gather along the shore. On its single street there are two rows of houses that huddle against the Caribbean winds to protect their inhabitants and one another. People in the village look like their houses—poor and crudely built and so tough they appear belligerent. No one will sell us any mussels, though we ask everywhere.

A large black woman is squatting in a doorway surrounded by her brood of children, hers and her neighbors'. She is selling something.

"Tell me," my friend asks politely, "are you selling mussels?"

"No," she mutters.

"Could you tell me where we can find some mussels?"

She grins. "On the bottom of the sea," she says.

* * *

On the water small fishing boats lay at anchor as gently as the morning light on the calm sea. A school of fish is in the harbor. The boats had gone out early, all together, before dawn, the kerosene lanterns tied to poles on the side of the dingies flickering on the dark water. Some of the fishermen have caught enough fish by sunrise to earn all the money they need and they have docked by the quay below the market to sell their fish and go home.

Children of the fishermen begin to bring the fish ashore. Some of the younger boys hold the fish by their tails, in their fists, like bunches of ripe bananas. Some of the older boys stand in the boats with their legs spread to balance themselves and toss the fish on the rocks of the quay. On the rocks squat groups of men who deftly cut up the fish, gut and bone them, and salt them in fistfuls of coarse sea salt. Each man works independently, in silence, and yet each man works together with the rest, as a silent team. In this way, as well, they cast their nets and man their boats and pull in their catch and market their fish, separately and together. In the port of Carúpano, or on the island of Margarita, wherever there are fishermen, this is their way.

In a few hours tons of fresh fish are in the market. No one can sort and prepare so many types of fish as fast as these men who squat here precariously on the quay. The skills of these fishermen are hundreds of years old. They've come from the Caribbean Indians who fished in these waters for many tens of thousands of years and from their African ancestors who fished off the coast of West Africa equally long ago.

The fishermen are black men, many of them, black of skin, if not black from the sun. Many of them are the descendants of African slaves who were abandoned by history on the remote seacoasts of lost memories.

On their black faces the fragile profiles of the Caribbean Indians and the blue eyes of their European masters subtly color their character; the inheritance of the seafarers of three continents—of America, Africa, and Europe—has shaped not merely their bodies but also their souls. It seems to have given them a resilience and ambiguity, as if they are the orphans of the sea.

A fisherman, on seeing me writing this, offers me a fish. When I politely decline the fish, he stands up, in anger, and faces me.

He tosses the fish into the sea and bids me to do the same with my manuscript. It is a gesture the meaning of which I do not understand. But, the other fishermen seem to know his meaning, for they all stand up, holding a fish above their heads, in a curious display of solidarity, though they do not throw their fish into the sea.

They laugh, though not at me. They laugh, I think, for the sheer pleasure of laughing together. After all, they were tribal men not too long ago. In the black villages they shared their lives and their common nets of fish. Even now when each man's family fishes for itself, they work together and not for another man. They are tribal entrepreneurs.

Some say that on Lake Maracaibo when the oil rigs that rise from the water were first built, the early work crews were recruited from these fishermen from the island of Margarita and the ports of Carúpano. That was because, an oil executive tells me, these black fishermen know how to work together as a family of men, as oil crews must do.

No, that isn't why, another oil executive tells me. It is simply that the fishermen were not afraid to work on the water. They know how to swim.

One of those tall tales of the sea, I thought, a fantasy that becomes a legend when men who live on land attribute a mysterious potency to men who live on the sea. That's all it is. Romanticism of the sea ennobled by the oil industry that needed heroic men, but had so few real heroes of its own. So it borrowed these.

And yet, as I see these fishermen on the quay, I wonder.

* * *

Seven drummers beating long, hollow African drums lead the solemn, but not so solemn, religious procession down the winding street of the village. They are handsome black men with Ashanti and Yoruba faces. On the shore of Lake Maracaibo, in the tropical heat of the noon sun, their faces glisten with the sweet sweat of rum as they beat the drums in the rhythms of their ancestors, brought across the ocean hundreds of years ago on the slave ships.

But, this is not West Africa. This is west Venezuela. No one in the village knows where the drums come from. And the beat of the music. And the rhythm of the dance. They say that these things have come from the memories of their ancestors. But, no one knows where and when.

The procession has come to a halt in the little plaza. Beneath a traditional brush shelter, made not of palm leaves but of corrugated tin roofing, the drummers take their positions in silence. The Master of the Dance, a village elder who has led them through the streets, tells them what the beat will be. He hums it. But before they can begin, the effigy of San Benito, the black saint, who was borne behind the drummers, has to be placed on his altar, a small table decorated with flowers and set in front of the general store of the village with its resplendent Pepsi-Cola sign.

An old man comes into the village plaza with a bottle of rum. It is given to a young man who goes from drummer to drummer offering each man a plastic cupful, which he swallows at once. The drumming begins again.

Once more the young man goes from drummer to drummer. They drink a second cup of rum, holding the cup in one hand while maintaining the drumbeat with the other hand. When the rum is gone a villager brings the young man another which he continues to offer the drummers. And when the rhythm of the drums is sufficiently invigorated by the rum and it is so intense and insistent the earth seems to vibrate, the young man begins to offer it to the villagers and spectators. None refuse, for it is impolite and a bad omen as well, not to join in the spirit of the dance.

Soon I have had two full cups. My feet have begun to dance to these black drummers, though I do not move my white limbs.

The dancing is begun by the Master of the Dance. He is a statuesque man, wearing a diplomatic sash of blue silk on his chest. In his hand he holds a sacramental cane, perhaps the symbol of his authority, with which he occasionally taps the earth sharply. As he dances, he lifts his muscular arms, as if they were heavy and broken, like an awkward bird, until he begins to take flight with the rhythm of the drums, his large body soaring and leaping with the grace of a gazelle; his dance is at once sensuous and dignified, as he circles about an old woman in a red turban who has joined him.

On his head he wears a straw hat, not an African crown of feathers. But, a single macaw feather is stuck in his hat-band. The dance is too public to be sacred and yet beneath that South American hat and those North American blue jeans his body is speaking an older language to a distant God.

Some of the old women then begin to dance. One by one their bodies move, slowly at first. Their hips sway modestly and their movements are deliberately muted and restrained. Nonetheless, their bodies are suggestive of what the dance is saying.

A younger man leaps into the dance with both feet; his dancing is vigorously erotic and masculine. So furiously virile are his antics that the old women smile as he prances around them. Some of them giggle. They are not so amused, however, by the amorous attentions of this young Lothario of the village that they are not flattered. Even the oldest women remember.

They are dancing in a celebration of the triumph of the living over the dead. It is a dance of life. No one is too old for such a dance. And these old women know the dance the best.

An old woman of the village who was almost dead and

who has come back from the dead is celebrating not only her return to life, but life itself. She has arranged the ceremony of thanksgiving for herself and whoever shares her rejoicing. Everyone in the village has been invited to share this blessing that San Benito has given her, for as he led her out of The House of the Dead, so he shall lead the dancers. They dance for him and for her and for themselves.

In the village it is said the woman was so ill no medicine could cure her. The medicine people of the village tried, but they could not. And so, she was sent to the doctors in Caracas. They too tried, but they too could not. So she prayed to San Benito. An offering was made in the old way, not in the church. Her prayers were answered. For this blessing the villagers will dance all day and all night, until they have danced death into the earth. They sing:

Ai, Ai, So do we live . . .
Ai, Ai, So do we live . . .

The beat of the drums has the rhymthic tempo that is heard in the national folksongs of Venezuela—the songs of the *llaneros.* It has a vivacious and melodious lilt which is not wholly African, nor uniquely American.

After all, these drums that resemble the tribal drums of West Africa were made of the trees of America. They have been carved from hollowed logs, from palm trees along the shores of Lake Maracaibo, in designs that give them the deep, resonant sound of ancient history. In the old way each of the drumheads is laced and tied down by thick, crude ropes which are knotted to pegs not quite at the bottom of the drums, where the ropes are further stretched by pegs so the leather is tightly held, as it usually is in the Caribbean.

Each of the black drummers beats out the beat with a small stick, as well as with his palms and fingers. One man plays a long flute, the kind the Andean Indian plays. One man has a large gourd rattle that he uses to punctuate the rhythm in a staccato style which might be either African or American.

No one knows the precise origins of this music. It is truly Afro-American, or more accurately, it is Latin and therefore Venezuelan.

On his altar San Benito listens to the music with silent eyes. His effigy is not large, no more than four feet tall, made of the white Catholic plaster of a lesser saint, and clad in a cheap cloth of light blue rayon and a bright purple cape. These are adorned with the simplest of crosses. But, he wears an ornate and resplendent array of sacred medicine amulets of gold and precious stones, so old that few know their origins and none will say. Some of these amulets may have come across the ocean from Africa in the old days.

Above the head of the black saint is a round tin disc. His halo resembles the flat round head of the West African tribal god of fertility, with his noncommital and smiling slits for eyes, and yet it strangely suggests, as well, the golden discs worn by the *caciques,* the chieftains of the *Arawak* Indians of the Caribbean and the Venezuelan coasts.

Is San Benito a deity of the Ashanti or Yoruba tribes of West Africa, disguised as a Catholic saint? Or, is he the *cacique* of the *Guájito* Indians who live off the far shore of the lake?

The ecstasy that celebrates these dances for San Benito is so erotic and joyous that it is not practiced within a church. His altar is a bower of tropical flowers and omens. And the dancing seems to a have an affinity with the hot sun and the rum. Even as the drummers talk to their drums, their drums talk to them in a language that is tribal and not European.

An old woman sits beside the effigy. Every so often she lovingly caresses and fondles his gown. She beckons me to come to the saint, not to kneel to him, but to embrace him. He is to be caressed.

Then a woman brings her infant son to the saint, face-to-face. And the child, lifting his hands, touches the hands of the saint, holds them, and laughs with delight. The old woman smiles approvingly. She is a medicine woman, the guardian not only of the saint, but of the ritual.

Now the drummers seem to be possessed. The sweat runs down their faces ignited by the rum and music. Still, the beating of the drums becomes faster and louder, as if from an internal fire. And even the old women begin dancing lithely and suggestively as young girls. My head is beginning to turn to jelly.

Ai, Ai, So do we live . . .
Ai, Ai, So do we live . . .

Either the drumbeat or the heat has become unbearable. It is difficult to distinguish between them. So I flee to the shores of the lake. There is a wooden pier, narrow and rotting, with many boards missing, that leads far onto the waters. A gentle breeze is blowing through the warm air, and though it is not cool it is soothing after that oppressive heat of the plaza.

On the moorings along the shore are several motorboats. And, all but hidden under the palm trees, are dug-out canoes, rotting in the sun. The village, from the pier, seems like any other built of whitewashed wood and mud houses, and yet on the farthest points of land there are two huts built of bamboo walls and thatched palm leaf roofs that look more West African than native Indian design.

"Were these medicine huts?" I ask the villagers. They only smile.

Once there were tens of thousands of blacks in the country, brought on the slave ships of the Dutch and Portuguese traders of rum and humans. Some say that there were one hundred thousand at least. The written records, as always, do not tell the whole story.

So many black slaves were brought from Africa that with the Indians they were the majority of the population. For centuries that was so. The Venezuelans were, as Simón Bolívar had said, the "mixture of Africa and America, rather than an emanation from Europe."

And from the beginning, when those first slave ships arrived in 1525, blacks and Indians were put to work together in the mines. Not long after these African slaves came, in the 1550s, the first slave revolt erupted in the gold mines of Buria and an army of blacks and Indians marched on the provincial capitol of Barquisimeto, arm-in-arm. Forever after, in colonial times, blacks and Indians were "hemmed in by restrictions governing their occupations, dress, associations, and movement within the cities or from place to place," says one historian. They were imprisoned within their cultures.

In succeeding years, slave revolts were savagely suppressed. By 1795, when a famous black rebellion began, its leader, José Chirinos of Coro, was not merely beheaded; he was drawn and quartered and his head and hands were taken back into the city where, as was the custom of the Spaniards, they were exhibited on pikes. Coro, curiously, was one of the oldest of the Spanish cities in Venezuela, and was settled by Sephardic Jews and converted Moors, who came to flee the Inquisition; it was a city of people who in origin were largely North African.

Few of them survived. There are no more than a half-dozen black villages left along the shores of Lake Maracaibo, where the great sugar plantations stretched for mile on mile. And on those islands and land of far eastern Venezuela, where sea pirates and smugglers traded kegs of rum for human bodies, the surviving blacks are hidden in small and obscure rural ghettos.

These sons and daughters of Africa have been submerged by the ways of life of modern Venezuela, it is said. Few have maintained the mother cultures of their homelands, and these few are living curios who contribute nothing more than exotic rituals for the diversion and amusement of the creators of the technological development of the nation. So they say the blacks are "negligible in numbers," and that they have offered little but color to the country.

And yet, on the waters of Lake Maracaibo, where their ancestors have fished for centuries, the descendents of the African slaves now work in the oil fields. They were among the first crews on the oil rigs, for being coastal people they knew how to swim and were not frightened by the danger of working high above the surface of the lake. And, too, being a tribal people who were accustomed to working together on their huge fishing nets that needed many hands working together in unison, they knew how to work as crews. And what was African, long ago, has become Venezuelan.

On the silent water of the lake I hear the drums echo. And the singing of the dancers comes across the waters, as from a distant place, far beyond the black village on the shore.

Refreshed by the water, I return to the dancing. Once more the young man with the bottle of rum is going from drummer to drummer; he is as mischievous as a sacred clown in a religious dance and on his face there is a devious grin.

Years ago, when their ancestors were brought here as slaves, they worked in the fields of sugar cane that surround the village, harvesting the sweet weeds the plantation owners brewed into rum. And with that rum the slave owners traded for more black slaves, in that strange man-made circle of life known as the slave trade. Even now it seems as if the drummers are not drinking the rum, but that the rum is drinking them; they are so drunk they do not seem drunk at all.

Suddenly, a small but sturdy dancer grabs me by my shoulders. His arms embrace me with affection and demand my attention. The rum glows in his black eyes. And he pulls me toward him.

"Brother, who are you?" he asks.

"A brother," I say.

"You are President Betancourt?" he asks in a joking voice, looking at my pipe. Betancourt, one of the founders of the modern constitutional government, is known for his pipe smoking.

"No," I laugh.

The man shrugs. "It does not matter," he says. "In Venezuela every man is the same color. Every man who is white, he is a little black. And every man who is black, he is a little white. Come to my house," he says. "And then we will eat together."

* * *

And so, who then are these people known as Venezuelans? These people who are not white, not brown, not black?

In his famous letter to the Congress of Angostura, the first constitutional congress of the country, the Liberator of South America, Simón Bolívar, in that ironic sense of history that was so peculiar to his character, wrote this penetrating observation of the psyche and the soul that was entombed in the flesh and blood of his nation:

We are the abominable offspring of those raging beasts that came to America to waste her blood and to breed with their victims (the Indians) before sacrificing them. Later the fruits of these unions comingled with slaves brought from Africa.

We must bear in mind that our people are neither European nor North American; they are a mixture of Africa and America rather than an emanation from Europe. Even Spain herself ceased to be European because of her African blood, her institutions, and her character. It is impossible to determine with any degree of accuracy to which human family we belong. . . . Europeans have mixed with Americans and Africans, and Africans with Indians and Europeans. While we have all been born of the same mother, our fathers, different in origin and in blood, are foreigners. . . .

So were born the people who now declare themselves Venezuelans. And so they will forever be, in body and in blood.

Requiem for the Countryside

A few years ago a young man came from the mountains of New Mexico to the flat equatorial plains of the savannahs of Venezuela. He spent a lazy summer on a cattle ranch on the Apure River. Ranch life was not unfamilar to him, for his family ran a small ranch in the Sangre de Cristo Mountains, the mountains of the Blood of Christ, north of Taos. But, that was a long, long way from roundup time in the Orinoco basin. That young man is Larry Vincent. And this is his memory of a way of life that is dying.

On the Llanos, the *llanero,* the cowboy of Venezuela, used to ride barefoot. And he did this by holding onto the stirrups with his toes. So his toes would become very strong and after he would lasso a wild bull, he would jump off his horse, run up to the bull, and stick his big toe in the bull's eye. Then the *llanero* would place his foot on the bull's face and he would proudly stand there. Naturally the bull would be surprised by all this and would lie there.

I had never seen that done before, not even in a country rodeo. So it amazed me, but it amazed the bull even more. But, the *llanero* had a kind of pride in doing things like that. He didn't pretend to be *macho*. He was.

These bulls were not the ordinary farmyard type of bull, you know. No, they came off the range and they were not inclined to look kindly on somebody sticking his big toe in their eyes.

The cattlemen on the Llanos do not castrate their bulls. So there aren't any eunuch steers. And the bulls grow strong and fiery as they wander freely across the open plains; they are spirited animals and not easy to round up. And so the *llaneros* must be equally strong and spirited. They are. Right down to their toes.

On the grassy savannah they may see a few bulls. The *llaneros* ride up to them very quietly and circle around them. Some go this way, some that way, until they have forced these bulls into an open clearing where they can lasso them. They use leather lariats made of twisted hide. It is the kind of lasso the Indians used to make in the old days.

When they have lassoed a bull they don't tie the lariat to their saddle. They tie it to their horse's tail. Like a rodeo horse, in calf roping, the horse will tighten up on the rope by turning and looking the bull in the eye. And that's when the *llaneros* begin hand wrestling or foot wrestling with the bull. They jump off their horses and grab the bull by the tail and throw it off balance. Once the bull is down on the ground, they rush over to it and stick their toes into its eye.

Riding barefoot is an old Indian tradition and it makes their toes as hard as knives. On the equatorial savannahs it still makes sense, for leather boots in the tropical heat are not only uncomfortable, they are unsafe in the snake-infested lowlands. Still, it requires great skill to grip the metal rings they use as stirrups between their toes.

Once I tried to ride barefoot. I could not do it; it was too painful. And I had to wear shoes. Men laughed at me, in their friendly way. "You are no *llanero,*" they said.

On the cattle ranch, or *hato,* where I was, we were so deep in the interior of the Llanos that the only way I could get there was by bush pilot. It's what they call a "milk plane," an old DC3 that lands at all those little towns way out in the savannahs. It's like the Old West out there. In some ways it's like it was a hundred years ago on the prairies, with the bush pilots as wagon masters.

These are not fenced ranges. They are open lands. A cattle rancher may say, "My land is up to such and such a place." And that's his land. He stakes it out by a hill or a tree and the other ranchers respect his boundaries. In those places, around the *hato* where they corral the cattle, there may be fences, but mostly it is a wide-open country. And the ranch houses look very much like the old ranch houses did. There isn't much luxury. It's a tough country.

Even the faces of the cattle come from the old days. Most of them are Longhorns, resembling the old Longhorn cattle of the early West, a mixture of every breed. They are known as *Criollos,* a *mestizo* stock, adapted to the tropical range, tough and scrawny. On the modern ranches they are being bred with Brahman, the cattle from India, to put some meat on their bones. These *Criollos* are like the *llaneros,* in some ways. No matter what happens to them, they somehow survive.

In the dry season there is no rain at all for three or four months. One can go in a jeep or ordinary car and drive right across the savannah. And when the wet season comes, much of the land is under water. Some areas are under water for six or seven months of the year.

And these Llanos are huge. One thousand kilometers of flat land that stretches from the foothills of the Andes to the Orinoco; nearly a thousand miles long and four hundred miles wide. Once in a while there may be a *mata,* a clump of trees, but mostly it is grassland, wild grass, not too high, that goes on mile after mile from the mahogany forests of the high Llanos up in the *Caparo,* all the way to San Fernando in the Orinoco jungles.

On my first morning on this ranch my hope was to ride out with the *llaneros,* on roundup. Everybody got up at four in the morning. In the dark. They have a cup of coffee and ride off. I thought somebody would offer me a horse. But nothing happened. They had their coffee and left me there. So later, I went out to their corrals where these *llaneros* were breaking horses. They were horses that grew up on the range, not too wild, but not too tame either. So I figured the only way I would ever get on a horse was to show them I could, but they told me these weren't "nice horses." And I said I knew that. They let me get on a horse, and the horse immediately threw itself on the ground. So they asked me if I still wanted to get on a horse. I really didn't. But I did. The horse took off running, a *llanero* on either side of me, joking and yelling. And I stayed on.

And so the next morning they gave me a mule to ride. In the dark, after our coffee, we saddled up and rode out on the Llanos, to round up the wild bulls.

On the Llanos it is cool in the early morning, so most of the *llaneros* wear a *ruana,* the cape the mountain people wear. But in spite of the cold they not only go barefoot, but wear their pants cut off just below the knee to give them greater freedom in the saddle. And they usually wear a large knife, like a kitchen knife, in a sheath on their belts.

In the grasses there are sometimes wild animals. There are always poisonous snakes. Even the bulls have been known to attack a man rather than surrender to his desire to eat them. These cattle stay on the range by themselves almost year round. The ranchers don't see their cattle and their cattle don't see any humans for months. So they become independent-minded; they call them *cimarrónes,* the wild ones.

On that day when I rode with these *llaneros* we had a hard time finding any bulls. It reminded me more of deer hunting than a cattle roundup. But we kept riding. Whenever the *llaneros* would lasso a bull they would mix him with a herd of oxen they brought along, and when they had caught several they drove the whole herd back to the corrals.

It was a long hard day. We had ridden out at five in the morning, in the dark, and we did not ride in until six in the evening, in the dark. Most often the *llaneros* will come in from the range at noon, for a big meal, but that day we were in the saddle for thirteen hours. Without any food. Without water.

No wonder these *llaneros* are the folk heroes of Venezuela. They are tough men whose lives are like legends of the past, living in our times. In the cities the *llaneros* have become the symbols of the Venezuelan spirit of independence, a mystique not unlike that of the western cowboy in the United States, but even more realistically so.

Songs of the *llaneros* are the national folk music. The myths of the *llaneros* are celebrated in the national literature. The history of the *llaneros* is considered the model of national patriotism.

And the *llaneros* are the heroes of the country's history.

They are celebrated as the most heroic soldiers in the War of Independence. In the armies of Bolívar, it was the *llaneros* who formed the most dashing and colorful battalions, the soldiers on horseback.

Once these men's bravado was the nation's strength. It is no more. But it seems to hold onto people's hearts. Most of Venezuela is still cattle country, even today. So, though young men may dream of being highly paid and skilled workers on the oil rigs by day, by night they dream of being poor cowboys. The *llaneros* are seen as the last free men.

Not until my last days of working on the ranch did I really experience the *llaneros'* sense of freedom. That was when we began separating the young cattle and the bulls, to prepare for a cattle drive to market. It began like an old western cattle drive, though it was not quite as long. For two days and nights we drove the herd overland, through the savannahs and across the rivers. On the banks of the Apure, a large river, the *llaneros* demonstrated the boldness for which they are famous. As they neared the river, at the crossing point, they stampeded the herd, driving the cattle as fast as they could so that they hit the water with a great splash. Then they got into dugout canoes and, pulling their horses behind them by their reins, they too crossed over.

Yelling and laughing, they entered the river like surf boarders. Some plunged in on horseback and rode the currents to the far side. A few cattle were swept downstream and lost. But very few.

On the far bank they drove the cattle to a slaughterhouse near an airstrip. There the bulls were slaughtered and dressed and flown to market. In celebration the *llaneros* killed a heifer. They ate the whole animal. They butchered it and roasted it on an open fire, piercing the chunks of meat on long sticks which they held in the flames until, by evening, the heifer was devoured.

That evening a restless but gentle wind came up. On the savannahs the sea of grasses began to blow endlessly over what once had been a prehistoric sea, where the Llanos now unfolded wave upon wave of its wild grass. Never have I felt as free as I did that evening.

That was long ago, even though it was only a few years ago. Now all of that has changed. Now we import beef. Now the *llanero* is going to the city where he is earning his living riding herd on pedestrians by driving a taxi. Now the closest he gets to a wild bull is the leather in his shoes.

He probably wears Italian shoes.

* * *

In a skyscraper in the center of Caracas are the offices of the Ministry of Agriculture. There are two security guards in the corridor. And the reception room is a sealed-off cubicle with glass walls and no windows. No sun ever shines into the room and the droning of the airconditioners drowns out any noises from the city streets. In the reception room of the Ministry of Mines there is a lump of iron ore, but here there isn't even a kernel of corn.

Three large men, cattlemen, sit awkwardly in the reception room waiting to be admitted to an audience with the Minister of Agriculture, Dr. Gustavo Pinto Cohen. One of them I recognize as Sr. Rafáel Marcial Garmendia, the President of the Federation of Cattle Ranchers. He is a powerfully built man, but he looks uncomfortable and boyishly ill at ease in the glass room.

One of the men says: "The cattle industry is not good. So we have to come to the government for help."

"And will you get it?" I ask.

"No," he says. "Just last year the government authorized the import of 150,000 head of cattle when the country consumes only 180,000 head. That is like importing oil to Venezuela."

"So why do you wait?" I ask.

"We are the orphans of the economy," he says. "All that orphans can do is wait."

The "Israeli Phenomenon," as economist Dr. Meir Merhav was known, had been brought to Venezuela to prepare a special report for the Ministry of Agriculture on the problems of the farmers. His thoughts were troublesome.

Merhav had warned that the set of dilemmas with regard to agricultural policy that began in 1974 had become more severe. Since that year there had been a significant erosion of real living standards in rural areas, he wrote, and the impoverishment of large classes of low income earners in the face of the new bounty derived from oil had led to an apparent discrepancy between the new wave of wealth and the reality of falling real standards of living. The poor were getting poorer and the rich were getting richer. But, the farmers were getting nowhere.

In the Ministry of Agriculture no one would discuss the report. They had never seen it, they told me.

One hour later that afternoon, after leaving my audience with the Minister, Dr. Pinto Cohen tells me that agricultural production has reached record levels in almost all sectors of rural life. The cattlemen are still waiting in the glass room. They look as though their heavy torsos have been butchered and tossed at random onto the overstuffed modern furniture.

"Everything is wonderful," I tell them happily. "You need not worry."

"That's good to know," one of them replies. "If the Minister is not worried about us, why should we worry?"

"I wish you luck," I say.

"No," one man smiles wryly, "do not wish us luck. You should wish it for the Minister. You know he is the fourth Minister of Agriculture we have had in four years."

"Why?" I ask.

"Ah!" he says. "It is easy to grow statistics. But it is harder to put meat on their bones."

The cattlemen sit there nodding. In his large hands one man has twisted his newspaper into a whip. He swats at an imaginary fly.

* * *

One man in a small village says to me: "Many people would stay in the *campos* if they could work their little bit of land and make a living on it. And they wouldn't go to the cities. But life is not easy in the rural areas. Not easy at all. There are few roads. And in the rainy season you can't use even those. There is no electricity. There are few jobs. There are few schools. If there is a school it goes to the third grade, or maybe the sixth grade. What kind of education is that?

"And everyone in the poorest village wants their kids to have an education," he says. "Why? Because that's how they get high paying jobs. So the children all leave the farms as soon as they can.

"Everything goes against the small farmer. To survive he must pay low wages, but when the economy changes to an industrial economy and people can earn high wages in the city, there is no way that a small farmer can survive."

Suddenly I feel that I am in a village meeting in northern New Mexico, or talking to a peasant in southern France. But no, this man is not talking about the traditional hard times on the farm. He is talking about the death of the small farm. He is talking about progress.

"On the small farms the margins of profit are so small, the farmer can't make a living," he says. "A few years ago a farmer who raised a few chickens could go to market and sell them and make a few dollars. Now it doesn't even pay him to sell them.

"I read in the newspaper that one freighter from West Germany brought eleven thousand tons of frozen chickens. And they sell them cheaper than we do. So we eat West German chickens.

"When you talk to the small farmers they will tell you they can't make it anymore. They can't sell their produce for as much as it costs them to grow it. They can't afford the price of equipment and seeds and fertilizer. They can't even get people to work on their farms. Maybe the government is now helping the big farmers. But no one helps a small farmer. It is no longer economical to have a small farm, they say.

"That's why I am moving into the city," he says.

*   *   *

In the quiet village of Santa Inés in the mountains of Baragua many of the houses are deserted. The people have gone to the cities. And in the single cafe on the town's single street, with its two bare tables, there are more chickens than there are customers. Sometimes farmers from the countryside will come in for a plate of meat and potato soup and sometimes young girls waiting for the bus to the city buy a Pepsi-Cola. Mostly the cafe, much like the street, is empty.

And I wave to the empty street and ask the woman who has brought our plates of meat and potato soup (the meat is mostly fat and gristle): "Tell me, where are all the people? Where have they gone?"

"To the city," she says.

In the days of the somnolent Gómez dictatorship, in the 1920s, the economy of the country had been "almost entirely" agricultural, one study said. So it was, as late as 1963, when the *Encyclopaedia Britannica* wrote that it was "a generally backward country in which 75 percent of the population was agricultural and pastoral." Forgiving the romantic English snobbery, "pastoral" and "agricultural" were not synonymous. And neither was necessarily "backward." In any event, most of the people lived in the countryside.

Now, it is said, more than 75 percent of the people live in the cities. Some say that 90 percent of the people have gone there, but some could not survive there.

And so I ask the woman in the village cafe of Santa Ines who stands guard over our table waving away the chickens as we eat our meat and potato soup: "Tell me, do the people who leave your village to go to the city ever come back again?"

She grins. "Oh yes," she says. "They come back. When they are dead."

* * *

On the silken sands of the shore the waves have washed the beaches white. They look that pure. Where the Caribbean eddies in quiet lagoons along the Bay of Sorrows there is a neglected beach resort hidden among the palm trees at the end of an unmarked, sandy road, where on weekends young lovers from the cities come to lie beneath the salty stars and dream that they are as naked as the sea and sky. To me it seems to be a paradisiacal place. And it is.

In the evening the palm trees gently bend to the wind from the sea. And the lights go on in the little open air restaurant and bar, flickering like fireflies because the electricity is weak. The evening air is warm and yet the twilight is cool. No one moves fast, least of all the waiters, but then, there is nowhere to move to. Even the sun seems to be taking an incredibly long time to set into the sea; a lassitude possesses me. And yet, the beach may not be as idyllic as it seems to me. After all, the showers in the cabins do not work, the electric bulbs are half dead, the screens are filled with holes, and the flies are as thick as beer cans on the beach. Still, sitting in a deep wicker lounge chair, while the sun sets beyond the palm trees, full as a round ball of naked flesh, I could easily be convinced of anything.

The serene scene has been slightly jarred, it is true, by the appearance of a five hundred foot high smokestack on the horizon, that rises from what is said will be the largest power plant in Latin America. It is a technological wonder of engineering beauty that is being constructed by Siemens, S.A., of West Germany. Once, in less idyllic places, Siemens was accused of developing and manufacturing the gas chamber installations used by the Nazis at Oswiecim and other death camps; the company had a monopoly of gas chamber electrical equipment.

But, on the Bay of Sorrows they are merely building an electric plant. Nothing more.

In the darkening sea, boys and girls with golden skins emerge, hand-in-hand, and vanish into the drowsy cabins which are strung along the beaches. The palm trees cast their shadows. No lights go on within the cabins.

On the edge of the waves sixteen young bulls have gathered on the beach for a nightly ritual that even they do not understand. The surf splashes about their hoofs, but the young bulls do not seem to mind, do not move, do not bellow, do not do anything. As they do every evening when the swimmers have gone, these young bulls stand by the water's edge, in meditative silence. Then one by one they lie down and go to sleep. In the morning they will leave, as they came, in single file.

The lights go on in the cabins of the young lovers. And the girls come out into the night, lifting their arms to embrace the dark with joyous abandon. And the boys come out sleepily and yawn. In the bar a band begins to play. Some couples drift toward the music. They dance awhile; they drift away. By midnight the music has stopped, and the dancers drift along the beach to their cabins and lock their doors.

Silence fills the night. There is darkness everywhere, but for the beautiful blue and red lights atop the smokestack of the power plant. I stand on the beach and admire the serenity that shines down on me from above. Somehow it seems as if the smokestack of Siemens, S.A., has reached into the stars and snatched these stars from the firmament to make a halo of colored lights.

One year or two from tonight the power plant will be built, the tankers will clutter the lagoon with petroleum, the waves will be polluted, the sky will be aromatic with chemicals, the beach resort will be abandoned, and the cabins of the young lovers will be empty.

And only the young bulls will come in their nightly ritual to stand in meditative silence at the water's edge, in the Bay of Sorrows.

* * *

Seven years of plagues as in the Bible.

For seven years a plague of rats has infested the Llanos. There rats are the descendents of the creatures who had spread the Black Death across Europe in the thirteenth century. But, on the Llanos they kill crops, not people. Not yet. Alejandro Urbaneja, the president of the Agricultural Association of Guárico says: "In Venezuela, as a whole, it is estimated that (the rats) have been responsible for destroying up to 80 percent of all crops planted."

A farmer tells a reporter for the *Caracas Journal:* "We never pick up dead rats. We just let them rot on the dams and in the water. They make good fertilizer."

On the Road to the City of the Urban Campesinos

On the country roads the women, at about noon, come from their huts. By twos and threes they slowly walk along the edges of the roads, going to the river for water. It is a stately procession that takes place every day in every village in the country; the pilgrimages of women to the springs and waterholes to bring water to their families, and using that most beautiful tool of rural technology, their own bodies.

It is lovely to see.

Some women carry the water pails on their heads. The older women do this with skill and dignity. Of necessity when a woman carries water in this way she has to hold her body straight and her head high. When a woman lifts the pail of water onto her head she holds the sides with her hands to balance it. And as she does so her breasts rise upward and her torso becomes statuesque. It is not a pose, but a simple matter of logistics.

To walk in this way a woman has to walk with the movement of her hips. They sway in undulating rhythm. Still, her torso maintains its dignity and poise as she does so; it has to or the water pail will fall from her head.

Not all of the country women carry water this gracefully. It is only the older women who wear loose dresses in the traditional style and who possess a freedom of movement beneath the cloth who can walk in such grace.

In their tight blue jeans and thin polo shirts the younger women do not seem to have the necessary ease. Their skin-tight clothing makes it painful to lift their arms above their heads and balance a water pail, for the fabric cuts into the armpits and in between their thighs. More troublesome is the embarrassment that it causes them. If the younger women do lift their arms, their small breasts are thrust upward against the thin cloth of their polo shirts and they feel undressed and defenseless to the men who sit by the roadside watching. When a woman in a village does this, the meaning is clear. So these younger women carry the pails of water in their hands. That is not easy to do upon the country roads through the mountains and jungles. Soon their hands become red and raw, as they struggle along, dragging their heavy pails. And they spill a great deal of water. So they have to go back for more.

But, the younger women are in love with their blue jeans and polo shirts. They dress like the women on the television shows they have seen. They walk like women in the cities of their dreams.

And, besides, carrying a water pail on your head is old-fashioned. It is the sign of backwardness, the curse of country life that they wish to escape from. So, they stumble heroically up and down the village roads with their bright colored plastic pails, awkwardly trying to spill as little water as they can. They are, in their effort to seem sophisticated, not without a certain pathetic dignity, but, urban fashions are ill-fitted to rural living.

In this village the pilgrimages of the women on the country road pass a store that sells bathroom fixtures, even though there is no running water in the village.

One of the younger women pauses in front of the store and rests her pail to gaze at a bathtub sitting in the grass under a palm tree.

* * *

One day a little girl, the flower of her mother's eye, becomes ill—so ill that she has to be taken to a hospital. The mother weeps and weeps. She is new to the city and she fears hospitals; she is a good woman, as they say, but simple—a country woman. Her skin is dark and her face is earthy. So, it seems, are her emotions. When the mother visits the hospital to see her daughter, she becomes hysterical, wailing and praying and beating her breasts. The daughter, too, begins to weep and wail.

Cool but friendly, a nurse who resembles one of Charlie's Angels comforts the mother and takes her aside. The nurse is blonde and light-skinned. She looks like a fashion model, but she knows all about the modern way to care for children, and so she teaches the mother how to be a mother, in a city hospital.

The mother obeys the nurse. And she goes away chastened. More precisely, she goes to a beauty parlor where her thick, dark, peasant hair is transformed into a sort of black Farrah Fawcett-Majors wig. Somehow her skin seems to have become lighter too. And so the mother becomes a new woman, or rather an urban woman, who is less emotional and more restrained. Evidently, though she was an illiterate country woman she has now learned to read, for she returns to her daughter's bedside with a book which she demurely opens and quietly begins to read aloud. Her daughter is delighted with her new mother.

And with this happy denouement this episode of the soap opera on Caracas television happily comes to an end. The commercial comes on, advertising a deodorant.

The evening that I watched this little morality play I was in a rural town, out in the *campos*. Even the poorest huts of the *campesinos* in that town proudly displayed a television antenna.

Charlie's Angels is a popular program in the countryside. It is called, *La Blonde Mujer—The Blonde Wife.*

* * *

A country woman is cooking several *cachapas* on an open oven made of mud and clay bricks, by the roadside. The oven stands beneath a makeshift brush shelter roofed with tin. A family of hogs, scrawny and filthy from rooting in the roadside garbage, searches beneath the bare tables and benches for leftover scraps. On one bench three Indian-faced men sit silently watching the woman cook, and watching us. People from the city do not often stop to eat among the hogs.

She has cooked several stacks of *cachapas*. The Indian pancakes, thick and sweeter than tortillas, have a subtle aroma. Beside them on the grill that is fashioned from a road sign are heaps of sizzling *chicharrones,* those crisp pork rinds that are fried to a tooth shattering hardness.

For a few centavos we buy an armful of *cachapas* and

chicharrones. And some *casabe* as well—those flat, hard biscuits that taste like dry cardboard. And some *queso de mano*, handmade country cheese in the shape of a small pancake. And with these native delicacies we are about to leave when the fat, dark Indian-faced woman calls out: "Hey, don't you want some Pepsi-Cola?"

* * *

She seems like a dream. In the dense tropical forest the bamboo hut of a *campesino* is half hidden by the trees. Amid the thick growth of vines and bushes, a young girl emerges from the doorway, in a frilly blouse, and walks along the edge of the road, a few feet back, displaying herself to the occasional man who may drive past, her head down and turned away, as if she is embarrassed by her loneliness. She walks back and forth for maybe an hour or so, then goes back into the hut. She seems to be walking in a waking dream.

Once again the young girl emerges from the doorway of the hut. This time she halts in the courtyard and leans against a tree; her eyes stare vaguely at the blur of the passing cars on the road and the faceless men who pass her by on their way to the city of her dream that she has seen only on television.

The young girl angrily kicks the dirt, frightening a chicken who runs into the road and is killed by one of the passing cars. She screams.

* * *

One of the vultures lies dead in the road. It has been hit by a car. The flock of mourners has gathered about it nodding their heads, pensively, as if uncertain whether it is proper for scavengers of the dead to devour a scavenger of the dead. Evidently the moral problem is too profound for them and they fly away to a nearby hill. On the hill there are hundreds upon hundreds of these vultures, waiting like black shadows for another death on the road.

The home of the vultures is in the suburbs of the city. It is surrounded by a garbage dump. Not far away, on the other side of the hill, there stands a motel for young lovers which is romantically hidden by the pastel shadows of the twilight that is descending upon the suburban scene.

On the mountain road that winds its way through the tropical forests of Lara, the green hills have unexpectedly given way to a bleak valley. Suddenly the earth becomes as red as dried blood. There are thousands of dying cactuses. Beyond this desert and the garbage dump and the hill of vultures and the motel for young lovers, chimneys of factories arise as far as the eye can see. And the city begins. The sky grows dim with smog in which lights of electricity shine like stars.

In the evening air the cows wander aimlessly amid the freightyards and parking lots. One cow, by the gates of a warehouse, is nibbling on a pile of discarded cardboard cartons and styrofoam packing crates, for there is no grass left where the farm of its owner had been. There is no farm either.

Once there was a provincial farming town in this agricultural valley. The country people came to sell their vegetables and chickens and to buy supplies and utensils. In those days the painter, Rafáel Monasterios, created a loving portrait of the town with its old colonial houses shaded with great green trees in the tones of Cezanne, the quiet scene protected by the watchful tower of the cathedral. That was the town of Barquisimeto in the year of 1944.

The provincial town has since become a city of maybe half a million or more. Like so many agricultural and mercantile centers it is a growing metropolis full of lost cows and country people who have come not to sell their vegetables and chickens, but themselves and anything else they can.

On the street corner outside the Commercial Hotel a little boy is trying to sell two packs of contraceptives he has stolen. "They are very good," he says. "They are American." A young girl comes by and lifts the receiver of the public telephone to see if there is a dial tone. She looks for any free change the machine may offer. An old man who shuffles down the alleyway, his eyes full of rum, is fingering the handles of the parked cars as he passes to see if any has been left unlocked by mistake.

No one buys the boy's stolen contraceptives. The young girl does not find any free change. And none of the car doors open in the old man's hand. And these three scavengers wander away. They will wait for another day.

* * *

On the new highways there may be an occasional dead dog by the roadside, or a burro that has been killed by some speeding car. Sometimes there is a writhing snake that has been partially crushed and left to die. There are dead iguanas. There are anteaters. There are armadillos. Once I saw an ocelot lying dead on the center white line, its lovely fur stained with blood, the victim of a Volkswagen bus.

The Rediscovery of El Dorado

"A man comes alone. If he finds a job he builds a *rancho,* a hut, with some boards and some tin and he sends for his wife. She comes with the children. But, the trouble is there may be six or ten or twelve children. Where do they live? They all live in the *rancho,* in one room, or maybe two rooms, sleeping or making love wherever they can—on the floor, anywhere. In the countryside they could sleep outside under the sky. But not in the city. So they have to sleep together. They never will be alone again."

The man who is talking is small and fatherly. He is talking about the country people who are coming from the forests into the city, and he speaks of them with compassion and sorrow, as if they are members of his family.

In the office building there are few, if any, quiet corners for a personal conversation. So we sit in the lobby of the massive structure with its huge cement blocks and glass windows that house the headquarters of the Corporación Venezolana de Guayana, the government agency which manages the new El Dorado on the Orinoco, a complex of some of South America's largest factories, mines, and hydroelectric dams. The small and fatherly man is one of the personnel directors of Ciudad Guayana, one of the greatest planned cities in the world, constructed from nothing, as they like to say, on the edges of the jungle highland of Guayana where a few years ago the wild jaguars roamed freely.

He is talking, not of these miracles of men, but of the men themselves. And his voice is intense and demanding. So I shall not interrupt him.

This is what he says: "On the *campos* the father was always a strong man. The children did as he told them. And the mother took them to mass in the church on Sunday. It was a very ordered life. But here the father is a little man in the big city and the mother—she is nothing. And besides, here the father is away from home each day, at work. It is not like in the *campos* where the father and mother always were the heart of the family and where the family always was close.

"So here there is no one to tell the children to behave. They do not go to mass. They have nothing to do here in the city, the way they did on the farm. They have only two things—stealing and politics.

"On the *campos* when something was wrong they would go to their father and to their priest. In the city they have a political protest. Politics is the religion of the young people in the city. They do not ask their fathers. And the family suffers because of such things. It comes apart. It has problems that are too big for it to solve. Most of all the fathers suffer.

"So, why do they come here? In the city the men have all

the things they ever dreamed about. Maybe in the countryside they had a better way of life, but they had nothing. Here they can have everything. When a man gets paid on Friday he can get drunk and have a woman. Every Friday he can get drunk and have a woman. The farmer, in the countryside, has to work for months until he harvests his crop and he gets a little cash, so he can go to the town and get drunk and have a woman. Here a man can do that every Friday night.

"And when the man sobers up he goes home and gives his wife fifty or one hundred bolívars (about twelve to twenty-five dollars) for the food for the week. Then he sleeps until Sunday.

"Even if he lives that way the man can buy a television. The antenna may be so big it collapses the roof of his hut, but he buys a television. Why? To see *Kojak* and *Baretta* and *Charlie's Angels* and *I Love Lucy*. Why? Because they really do love Lucy.

"These are country people who never lived in a city before. So to them it is all like magic. It is all overwhelming to them. Most of them do not know how to live in a city and they think that this is the way to live. It is what they have learned from television. Besides, the man here in Venezuela likes the good life, the easy way of life. He does not like to think about what will happen tomorrow. He lives as if there is no tomorrow."

The personnel director has talked for a long time. Now I do interrupt him and I ask him: "But what about tomorrow? If the people live on the country's resources as they are doing, what will happen when they are gone? What will happen to the people?"

A sweet smile lights his face for the first time. He enunciates an old faith in the circle of life which seems almost tribal. He says: "If our natural resources were to disappear tomorrow—all our petroleum and iron and everything else, you know what the people will do? They will say: 'Well, the cities are no good anymore. So let's go back to the countryside.' And that is what they will do. They will go back to the countryside, to the *campos*. And they will take their television sets with them."

* * *

"No one really lives here," says a technician who works for Siderúrgica del Orinoco, or Sidor as the steel mill is called. "They just work here. They work side by side but they don't touch each other. People aren't really neighbors; it is as if they just come here to work and make some money, they don't come here to live. So they are like strangers on the road. If a man wants to enjoy life he goes somewhere else on the weekend. Anywhere. There is nothing here.

"The man who is single gets drunk after work so he can forget his work. And then he goes to his room and goes to sleep so he is sober in the morning and ready to go work again. And the man who has a family goes home after work and locks his door and watches television until he goes to sleep with his wife so he can forget his work, and in the morning he is rested enough to go to work again. The man in the mill has to live to work; he doesn't work to live.

"No one can touch anybody here," the technician says once more. "This is no way to live."

* * *

In the offices of the steel mill, a man from the public relations department has brought me a bright orange hard hat made not of steel, but of plastic. The hard hat is the symbol of a modern man. And men not only wear it all day, they wear it home at night, not just for protection, but as a sign of pride. So I put on my plastic hard hat, for the man from public relations is going to guide me on a tour of the awesome and majestic steel mill.

Politely he asks me: "Now, tell me what I can tell you. Do you wish to know the production statistics?"

"No, I know them," I say.

"Then what is it that you wish to know? How can I help you?"

"I would like to talk to the workers about their work. Why have they come here? Do they like their work? How do they feel about it?"

"No," he says, "you cannot talk to the workers. That would interfere with production. I am sorry."

"May I talk to the machines?" I ask him.

He does not smile. My tour of the mill is cancelled. And I give him back his plastic hard hat.

* * *

Mira! Mira! Once there was a small village by the name of San Felix that drowsed in the sun of the savannah. It bothered no one. No one bothered it. For it was simply a sleepy river town with no more than a few thousand souls, a poor church, and poorer merchants who had no pretension of heaven on earth. Sometimes an adventurer did come searching for El Dorado. But it was generally thought that these strange men were mad men. No one in the village ever imagined that the mad men would ever discover anything. But they did.

On the day I came to San Felix a newspaper from Caracas reported the discovery of a half billion tons of bauxite (aluminum ore) in the nearby mountains. The mountains of iron ore and reservoirs of petroleum tar were already known throughout the world. Even the villagers began to believe the legends of riches the mad men talked about. And so the search began. Soon the village became a village of three hundred thousand people. Maybe even more. No one knows for sure. Everyone heard about the El Dorado that these mad men said they had discovered and so they wanted to see it for themselves. It was, after all, on their land. And so the people came to the village from miles around until it became perhaps the largest village in the world.

Mira! Mira! Where was El Dorado? The villagers searched everywhere. But, they could not find it.

For mile after mile along the river the banks are lined with the mud and tin huts of the villagers. The Brahma bulls wander up and down the dirt streets. In the plaza a huge hog is rubbing its rump on a junked car that has been abandoned in the middle of the street. A man stumbles out of an alleyway in between the huts and decorously pulls up his trousers; he seems unaware that the seat has been completely torn open, exposing his dirty ass to the bypassers, and walks with dignity into a *barrio* bar to watch the President of the Republic greet a foreign head of state on television. Little boys in the street run after the man pointing to his vulnerable parts. No one in the bar notices. A chicken, standing on the television set, dirties the screen.

Mira! Mira! In the yard of a hut a woman is cooking *cachapas*. Her daughter, sitting just inside the doorway, is nursing her baby. She has a bottle of Pepsi-Cola in her free hand and she is sucking from the bottle with a louder gurgling than her baby at her breast.

Mira! Mira! These villagers have not come to live in the city. No, they have brought their villages with them. And they live in their villages, in the city, in the way they did in the country. And they may dream, but do not believe, that they will ever enter the El Dorado of the mad men. No matter. It is good to be near the magic of El Dorado, even if they never enter.

Mira! Mira! Where was El Dorado? They can see it. They can almost touch it. But they cannot reach it.

On the far side of the river is Ciudad Guayana. But the villagers are not allowed to live there. They can see the chimneys of the factories rise into the sky, like missiles to the moon. But the villagers cannot enter them unless they can get a job in the factories of El Dorado, and so the magic is out of their reach.

Mira! Mira! In the gutters of a city street two little brown girls in torn dresses are lying amid the beer cans, in the dirt, in the heat, with their arms spread wide as if they are asleep, or pretending to be dead. A naked baby boy crawls about in the dust. He is their brother so they ignore him until he begins to climb over them. Then they jump on him, and pull on his penis to punish him, until he begins to cry at this indignity and he urinates on their hands. And he smiles in triumph.

One of the girls picks up an empty beer can and puts it over her brother's penis. He grabs it from her hands and tosses it into the street. The beer can rolls down an embankment of the Orinoco River where it comes to rest amid thousands of beer cans that line the riverbank. In the rainy season the high tide on the river will wash the beer cans downstream, to the sea. For miles and miles along the river the beer cans glisten like diamonds.

An elderly man comes to the door of the ramshackle hut. He speaks to the children in a soft voice. He says, "Why do you do that?" Then he goes back into the darkness of the hut. As soon as the man has gone inside, both of the little girls find new beer cans in the gutter. They squat on them and piss into them and then they throw them at their baby brother.

They seem to have played the game before, for the naked boy laughs and tosses the beer cans into the street and they roll down the embankment to the piles of beer cans that line the banks of the Orinoco, just below El Dorado.

Mira! Mira!

* * *

"El Dorado, which the Spanish conquerors so avidly sought in the sixteenth and seventeenth centuries, is now coming true, though quite differently, taking the form of iron ore, steel mills, hydroelectric development, aluminum, and a boldly conceived new town," says a proclamation of the Corporación Venezolana de Guayana. It is the "key to the development of Venezuela." It is "the cornerstone of Venezuela's progress." It is "the land of tomorrow." It "promises a better future which is already making itself felt."

One of the planners of El Dorado is Claude Brun. The manner of the man is skeptical and knowledgeable—two signs of long experience in attempting to plan for an unplanned society. He is a lean and lithe-minded man whose opinions of the city that he is designing are less enthusiastic, to say the least, than those of the official euphoria. To him it is no utopia.

And he tells me this: "There is a megalomania here. Every day there has to be more and more. Everything has to be the biggest, largest, greatest. It is a megalomania. I, myself, am responsible for the planning of the city. I, myself, would do it differently, planning for the needs of the people as well as the industry. But the planning is one thing. And what is done is another thing.

"Always industry comes first. In Ciudad Guayana, always industry has come before anything else. Before the needs of the people. Before the needs of the environment. Creating an environment for the people to live in is more difficult to do than creating an industrial factory. And so it is easier to build a factory than a human society.

"Sometimes they say that this is one of the greatest cities in the world created from 'nothing.' There is a great worldwide interest in what is happening in this city—an academic interest because it is the most planned city, even though it is not well planned. The city has grown like a mushroom; a mushroom city.

"In the early years, back in the fifties, the government began to draft a comprehensive plan for the city. The multinational corporations like Bethlehelm Steel and U.S. Steel, at that time, obtained mining concessions from the government. And these companies began what is typical of making a profit from an empty and undeveloped country. Company towns. No more than was necessary for them to exploit the mines.

"And so, when the government authorities came from the capital, later in the sixties—it was in 1961—and they said: 'We are going to found a town,' they did it on the old company towns. They hired experts from MIT, from the

United States, to begin planning the town. And the experts made their proposals and they went away. They did their best. But planning is not simply making plans on paper, all those bright, glossy plans in beautiful colors. It is also living.

"But, the truth is that industry always came before the people. It did then. It still does. Now we cannot cope with the explosion of growth. If we could slow down the growth of the town maybe we could cope with it, but on the national level they say we cannot slow the growth of industry. It is difficult for our country, in the petroleum crisis, a positive crisis, to think about slowing down. It is very difficult. So, as long as we have money, the growth will go on.

"And you know, it seems to me that there is confusion between growth and development. The word growth is an invented word. In Venezuela, they always speak of growth, but not development, and the fact is we have growth without development. They are not the same. If they thought about it they would wish development, not simply growth. But I do not know if they think.

"Here in Venezuela we are trying to develop in a few years what it took England centuries to develop. And so we are trying to buy the technology of the developed countries. But, I do not think you can buy human development. Ciudad Guayana is very typical of this. It is not a town. It is merely a place to work.

"When the country people come to the city they have no place to live. No one gives them any housing. They have to build their own houses. They have to become squatters. On the first night in the city, when a family puts four posts—sticks—in the ground and a tin roof over that, the unwritten law is that no one is permitted to pull down that house. The house, if it has no roof, well, you can discuss that with them. But, once the roof has been put on, then no one can put it away. It belongs to the family.

"That is the 'squatter's right.' Not that he owns the land he lives on; he only has the right to live there. He owns nothing. But if the government is after the land where he lives he must be paid for his 'squatter's right.' After all, what is the right of property? It is the piece of paper. If you have no paper, you have no right of property. In the system of squatting they have no paper. They just have the land.

"So, almost all of the people in San Felix are squatters. The government has managed to segregate the people on the other side of the river. If you are poor you live in San Felix. And so, we have two towns. We have two social systems, as every developing country does. There is a great river between the two towns and social systems.

"In some ways this might be the most segregated town in the world. The officials have decided to keep it that way. Whether this segregated city is a desired development of the officials is difficult to say. But, that is the way it is here. El Dorado! The mythical El Dorado! That is our El Dorado!"

And listening to the city planner describing his city, planned for industry and not for people as he says, I wonder why he lives in it. He is not simply critical of it. He is pained by it. When I ask him how he survives the pain he clearly feels, he surprisingly begins to laugh.

And he says with a shrug: "But, of course, I do not live in Ciudad Guayana or San Felix. No, I live in the old provincial capitol of Ciudad Bolívar. That is more than one hundred kilometers away. And I go back and forth almost every day. Why? Because I love old towns. For me it is very, very important for a human being to identify oneself with something that is old. Something traditional. Something of history, like an old wall.

"To live in surroundings like this where everything is new, in this El Dorado, I would not feel well. I could not live in this El Dorado. I need old walls."

* * *

The magnificent ruins of a great civilization that has hardly begun rise from a grassy savannah. It is an exotic and mysterious sight. As far as the eye can see the skeletons of highrise apartment houses, some of them twenty stories tall, stand abandoned before they are finished, the cement and steel buildings decaying in the tropical sun like the bones of gigantic dinosaurs. Even the shopping centers are desolate and empty as pillaged temples.

One apologetic official explains that the builders ran out of cement. The supplies of cement must go for the building of factories and dams. So, the houses for people must wait, for there is a shortage of cement.

In these days everything is speeded up. Even the creation of ruins.

* * *

The grass is gray. It is the dry season and it has not rained for months. On the horizons dust rises in the wind, like a flock of silent birds, but it is merely a jeep on a lone, long dirt road over the savannah that seems as lonely as the landscape of west Texas. And then, miraculously, the barren land has grown bright with row upon row of little green and bushy pine trees, as if the hand of God has scattered the wrong seed on the wrong planet.

However, it is not God, but man, who has planted the pine forest. There are eighty million pine trees where a few years ago there were none. Every day almost half a million more trees are sown. In a few years there will be one hundred and sixty million trees here.

Los Piños is one of the "natural" man-made wonders of the world. In these forests there are deer and foxes though none were here before. Nor has somebody brought the deer and foxes to the forest; they have simply come on their own. And the word has spread, for the forests are full of animals who were never known on the savannah before. There is an entirely new world of nature where nature had given up the world.

On the savannah, deep in the forest, is the work camp of Ovierto. It too is a project of the Corporación Venezolana de Guayana. In the forest the native people have not been driven from their homes; they have been given newer, larger homes and have been offered work if they wish to work on machines rather than upon their knees. Some prefer to continue raising their corn and hogs. They do not disturb the forest nor does it disturb them.

In a secluded glen where the river Uracoa slowly flows to the sea, there are groves of cashew trees. The water is pure and cool and clear. People bathe in the shaded pools surrounded by the factories of trees that cover the earth for almost half a million acres. These trees will supply wood products to the nation for generations, for in its way Los Piños is a gigantic industrial enterprise. And yet it is a "natural" world unto itself, an ecosystem of its own.

The steel mills of Ciudad Guayana cannot be seen from the forest. But they are not too far away. On certain days the smoke from the factories is visible upon the horizon. So far the smog has not injured the pine trees.

Sr. Fernando Gonzáles says to me as we drive through the pine forests in his bucking jeep: "No, here we have harmed nothing. And no one." And he smiles to himself. "But who has ever been harmed by the sowing of a seed?"

* * *

On the river ferry, the *Carabobo,* as we cross the Orinoco returning from the pine forests to the factories of Ciudad Guayana, there is an old man in torn Levi's and a battered hat who hands me a religous tract entitled: "Who Has Killed The Burro?"

"I do not know," I say to him.

The old man stares at me, startled to hear the strange Spanish from my mouth. He studies me for some time before he answers.

"People," he says.

Seven Wonders of Caracas

It is a gala celebration for the grand old man of South American democracy, the founder of the modern constitutional government, and the leader of the Revolution—former President Don Rómulo Betancourt. The Symphony Orchestra of Venezuela tunes up as the cream of Caracas society enters the Municipal Theater. These red carpets, red seats, red draperies, and red velvet walls have never seemed more regal. In his seat, the Cardinal nods to the President who rises to a standing ovation. Several generals, all in a row, beam their benediction.

The *Concierto Extraordinario* is about to begin and the Man of Honor comes to the podium. "That you think me a good man," he says, "is kind to an old man." It is a moving moment, the venerable warrior on his seventieth birthday, his voice firm and determined, his legs weak and unsteady, proclaiming once more his faith in the democratic credo of the Republic, its fight for social justice, its concern for the miseries of the poor.

"Now, you must not think of Venezuela as the Alice in Wonderland of South America," Betancourt admonishes his audience of the cream of society.

And the audience laughs. Is it a joke? They seem unsure.

* * *

Once, at twilight, the skies above the city were like the paintings of the Adoration of the Virgin. They still are. Few these days, however, see any virginity in the neon-lit skies. No longer do the evening breezes from the mountains blow away the sensual heat of the day in cool absolution. If they did they would surely be sucked into the air-conditioners of the new office buildings. The evening's breezes, if there are any, come most often from the rush of traffic on the *autopistas,* the superhighways.

The evenings are so sublime that in the old days Caracas was known as the City of Eternal Spring. And the settlers from Europe built their homes about portals and patios and verandas in the fresh air, beneath the heavens, as did the native people who originally settled in the then sacred mountains.

In the courtyards of the old colonial houses the sky has now stagnated. The silence in the patios has the sweet and sour odor of history. On the narrow streets in the older quarters of the city, the memories of yesterday are hidden behind the hand-carved wooden bars on the windows, like the shadows of the old women who peer from the darkness of their sanctuaries, lighting candles for forgotten saints.

On the sidewalks the old men sit on small wooden chairs, as if waiting for the evening breezes that will never come again. The old women laugh at them.

From the old quarters there rises a rancid aroma. It smells like a basket of tropical fruits left too long in the sun, the taste of a baby's warm flesh, the decay of death, the sweat of sex, the incense at the altar, the burnings of candles, the perfumes of orchids. To me it has the fecund and rich odor of life in the City of the Sun, as intoxicating as warmed rum to my nostrils, much like the nectar of myrrh and frankincense in the Old Testament.

But, the traffic on these streets, the roaring of the Japanese motorcycles and the farting of the American cars, obliterates these biblical odors. Instead, the smell of the exhausted pipes of the vehicles satiates the eyes, the ears, the mouths, the minds. In the evenings these are now the breezes of the city. They blow like blasphemy through the streets.

Once a "sleepy colonial town," the city has become a "sophisticated international city," a "pulsating metropolis"; it is "one of the most modern cities" in the world, says the Ministry of Information and Tourism. It is all true. There is no boasting or bravado in the superlatives that describe the "miraculous growth" of the city from a provincial capital of one of the backward nations of South America to one of the most spectacular monuments to instantaneous urbanization. Every morning it seems as if a new skyscraper has risen toward the heavens.

No one sits leisurely on the verandas anymore, for there are no verandas and there is no leisure. The shaded portals that have escaped the notice of the bulldozers have been remodeled into shopping centers. The old patios, where once gracious palm trees swayed, are now parking lots.

Day by day the old houses and the old women and the old men vanish. In the few months between my visits to the city entire blocks have disappeared, old *haciendas* have vanished, and a whole park has been devoured by the bulldozers and has been swallowed by the maw of the metropolitan subway. But the sorrow is not mine alone. The old women squint out upon the street scene in sorrow and disdain. And they withdraw behind their rosaries into the shadowed corridors of their memories where they inscribe a sign of the cross of Christ's sacrifice upon their martyred breasts.

The old women are too old to cry. So, they curse instead. One old, old woman says: "They are building a city without God."

"Why do you say that?" I ask.

"Because they are building a city for buildings, not for people!" the old, old woman says. "Without people there is no God."

"That's blasphemy," I say to her.

"Isn't the city?" she says.

Somewhere in an empty lot, where once a house stood, a breeze comes from nowhere and blows the remnants of past memories in circles around a deserted patio. Beneath the rubble are the lives of thousands of old, old women, buried alive. In the ruins their voices whisper like the evening breeze which no longer blows, asking in silence: "City of God. City of Technology. City of Buildings. City of People. City of Eternal Spring. City of Heaven. City of Purgatory. City of Hell. City of the Future. Which will it be?"

In the eye of my memory I see an image of the City of the Future arising from the fading past. Somehow this city reminds me of the Futurama exhibit of General Motors, built for the World's Fair of 1939, for it too was called the City of the Future. My boyhood memory of that fantastic, almost science fiction model of a city, was that its most memorable feature was its huge skyscrapers which towered above its tiny, nearly invisible people, who were connected to the city by umbilical cords that were called superhighways that led to clusters of buildings that were called shopping centers. These words, as I remember, had just been invented.

And Caracas, in many ways, seems a larger-than-life model of that City of the Future. It, too, seems to be an architecturally immaculate conception. For, as I remember it, the Futurama was created behind glass so that its skyscrapers were enclosed in an air-conditioned atmosphere untouched by history. These skyscrapers, too, have no human faces. Nor are they tropical. Inside their air-conditioned rooms there are no smells, no sounds, of the city beyond their walls. The old, old women may curse. But no one hears them.

In the sky above the skyscrapers then, one evening, the clouds open and the sun shines like a fiery omen to light the way of Christ as He descends from heaven into the city, upon the wings of His glowing halo of neon, like a holy helicopter landing on the roof of a majestic and quivering skyscraper. There is a sudden and terrible evening breeze that rises and sweeps the city away.

And, that evening, the sky is once more like the Adoration of the Virgin. And the old, old women cross themselves, and light a candle.

* * *

One evening at Maiquetía airport while waiting for my luggage, I meet a young man who is returning to Caracas after three years in Los Angeles where he was studying for his Ph.D. in mathematics at the University of California. Now, with his degree in hand, he is coming home to a high paying position with a government ministry.

"You must be a very happy man," I say to him.

"To tell you the truth I am very much afraid," he says. The solemn look in his dark and large eyes emphasizes his words. "In the morning when I got on the plane, I became afraid."

"Of what?" I ask.

"Here!" he says. "Of this city. I was born here. I grew up here. But now, everyone who lives here is a foreigner to everyone else."

* * *

In the evening the young couple strolls through the shopping center as though it is a tree-shaded plaza clustered about a church, rather than a parking lot. Between a Ford Pinto and a Dodge Dart the young lovers embrace, seemingly oblivious to the neon light that illuminates them. She fondly holds him about the waist of his blue jeans, while he holds her fiercely about the seat of her blue jeans. Even as he embraces her with one hand his other hand holds onto a hot dog and she feigns kissing him so that she may steal a bite.

And so the embrace of the young lovers becomes a playfully erotic game in which their prize is not an orgasm in the parking lot, but the hot dog. They behave as though it is an aphrodisiac to them. Maybe it is, for the struggle for the hot dog is sensual and intense, and they devour it from both ends with entwined limbs until their mouths meet with a kiss.

Surely a parking lot is a strange place for such passionate embraces. But, the young lovers seem excited by its very strangeness.

No one seems to see these young lovers' game of love. The passersby walk on with embarrassed and amused eyes, but they do not turn their heads. It is not proper to notice such things in public. And laughing, the young lovers lick each others' lips. It is, I think, a movie they once saw on television.

The scene is a shopping center in Caracas. But, it could be anywhere in the country from the suburbs of Mérida in the Andes to the dusty highway in Anauco, deep in the savannah. Everywhere the boys and girls from the country come to these new shopping centers to seek their new urban identities.

And they gather in solemn joy as once they went to church for the fiesta of their saint's day. They come to seek absolution from their backward country ways. They come to find the promises of heaven on earth. No wonder there is often an air of celebration in a shopping center, as if it is a festive and magical place where miracles may materialize before your eyes for the price of a magic garment or a mouthful of manna from the fast-food counter. It offers a new religion of instant gratification without even a confession.

In place of the poor *barrio* cafe there is the Baby Scotch Pub. Here boys who wish to be real *machos* drink whiskey from America, not rum from the *campos* that turns men into *campesinos.* There is a men's clothing store that sells English suits, called the Adam's Men's Shop. And there is a women's clothing store called Eve's Shoppe that sells silk negligees from Paris and Rome. One Scotch whiskey and one negligee will transform a boy and girl from the Third World into the man and woman of the first world.

The shopping center is no ordinary marketplace. It is a merchandiser of magic, a bazaar that is as exotic as any in the Arabian nights, and the temple of its conjurers is its supermarket, the CADA.

Here, in the CADA, there is a cornucopia of once unobtainable, if not forbidden fruit: a *fabulosa fragancia,* Babe Perfume de Faberge, that is so *sensual y extraña,* sensual and foreign; Brut *por el hombre,* so *viril en la noche; el Scotch de* Something Special; a *Gigante Verde,* Green Giant *corn de la crema;* Kellogg *tostadas de maiz,* corn flakes; and Cheez Whiz *pimentón;* Heinz *guayaba* baby food; Kraft *mayonesa;* Colgate *dental crema;* Lux *en excamas;* Moddess *positiva protección por la mujer;* Shaeffer pens, *una revolución en su mano,* a revolution in your hand; Pepsi-Cola *grande;* and Power Elite aluminum *basebol batas,* not to mention frozen chickens from West Germany, frozen fish from Japan, frozen beef from Argentina, and frozen TV dinners from the United States.

But, by far the most magical place in the shopping center is not its CADA. It is Le Drugstore. Le Drugstore is the meeting place of the young lovers. It is the Venezuelan imitation of the Parisian imitation of the California phenomenon, with strobe lights, mirrored walls, psychedelic color, and loud rock music. From its fast-food counters come those exotic and erotic dishes, the two-foot-long hot dogs and the *tropic hamburguesas.*

In the parking lot the embrace of the young lovers has been torn asunder by the pangs of hunger and their bodies separate to satiate themselves, not with one another, as they go hand-in-hand into Le Drugstore. They will undoubtedly order another hot dog.

On this evening some street singers have wandered into Le Drugstore. A long-haired young man, his blonde tresses reaching his waist, his wife and four little children with washed faces, shiny as a Nebraska day—these street singers are refugees from the Peace Corps. They sway to the awkward rhythm of the young man's guitar as they sing a Venezuelan song in the earnest Spanish of their Anglo voices, more Venezuelan than the Venezuelans.

The Caracas youth who have come to the shopping center to become anglicized listen to these street singers with unbelieving eyes. And when the Yankees, so full of Latin rhythms, have finished their performance and go from table to table begging for a few *centavos,* the patrons of Le Drugstore reward them with stares of confused bemusement.

"Isn't that nice," says a Venezuelan girl at my table as she goes on eating her hot dog.

* * *

The dark brown-skinned woman has majestic black hair which has been elaborately waved in a beauty parlor. She looks handsomely African in spite of it. Her eyes are deeply black and her neck is like that of a dark brown swan. On her lithe breasts she is wearing a polo shirt of bright orange that emphasizes the suppleness of her brown body rather dramatically. And on the polo shirt, where it is stretched across her nipples, are the words, in English: "Gentlemen Prefer Blondes."

Is English erotic? The language of Hollywood, it must be. Not the meanings of its words, for the young woman cannot read them, but the words themselves. Simply because they are in English they possess the powers of a fertility fetish, the sexual powers of a sensual amulet that hangs around the neck for everyone to see. The polo shirts of the young women are rarely, if ever, inscribed with Spanish words. English has become the language of exoticism.

In magazines the word for love is *amor,* but the word for sexual things is "Sexy," written in English. The allure of sex is seemingly made more alluring by an English spelling; as if sex has become another foreign product imported from North America.

So, the young girls now wear polo shirts that say, in English:

Farrah Fawcett-Majors
I Love You
Kojak, I Love You
Property of the Los Angeles Rams
Star Wars
What Are You Looking At?

One young girl is wearing a polo shirt with the words, "I Want It," on her back. And on the front, across her small breasts, it says, "I Got It." She speaks no English. Nor does her friend, whose polo shirt has the single word, "Erotic," emblazoned in red over her left breast, so her nipple is visible in the O.

* * *

The elegant and gigantic towers of the Parque Central form one of the great building complexes in the world. It rivals the architectual wonders of Brasilia, of the Kremlin, of Rockefeller Center, of the hanging gardens of Babylon. Nothing has been spared in the lavish creation of these financially and aesthetically majestic monuments to the glorification of city life. But, somehow, the architects have forgotten to build sidewalks in front of the buildings.

Anyone who wishes to walk, if only to stroll beside that superhighway which runs before the buildings, has to dodge the limousines and taxis. After a year of accidents the street is divided by stanchions, half for the cars and half for the people.

On the cement viaduct that crosses the superhighway, I stroll in the evening, enjoying the psychedelic lights of the traffic.

A man ran across the highway yesterday, just below. He dodged the cars as though they were wild horses. It is a popular sport in the city, where crossing a street is a feat. They killed him.

"Our city is being built for cars, not for people," a director of the Parque Central explains.

My rooms, where I am staying on a top floor of the building, are a smaller suite. There are only five rooms, a sitting room and dining room and full kitchen and laundry, and two upstairs bedrooms; it is a duplex with two bathrooms and a balcony. But, in the kitchen there is an unnerving sign: "Dear Guests: We suffer periodic water cuts in this part of the city. We ask you turn on your taps and no water comes out you immediately shut off. Otherwise when service is restored flooding will occur."

There was no water, I am told, for a week or more last year. In a country of tropical rains that seems strange, but it was stranger still to see the guests in the luxury hotels bathing themselves in the luxurious swimming pools. At least they were cleansed by chlorine.

A woman who remembered that week without water shuddered: "Can you imagine," she says, "those unwashed bikinis drying in the wind of the airconditioners, in the duplexes. Thank God for the electricity."

On the evening that I left there were lines of parked trucks before the entrance bringing in television equipment that had been specially flown in from the United States to film the visit of President Carter. He arrived the following day. And a vast and intricate communications center was set up in the empty swimming pool.

But, the following day the Parque Central and the entire section of downtown Caracas was darkened by an electrical power failure. It was not sabotage, an official said; it was "fate." Perhaps it was.

* * *

Never is there enough of anything and yet there is too much of everything. There are too many people in the cities and too few houses for them to live in. There are too many cars on the streets and too few who know how to drive them. There are too many modern bathtubs and not enough water to fill them. There are too many television sets and not enough electricity to light them. And there is too much wealth and too little work. It is known as "The Law Of Too Much and Too Little."

Some call it "The Caracas Law," but it is common to all developing countries in the Third World.

* * *

"Once the people from the *campos* come into the cities they always forget their traditional ways," an anthropologist says to me. She shakes her head in sadness, almost in mourning. "It is very tragic," she says. "Centuries of native culture are lost in a single generation. Why? Because the cities are the cemeteries of the culture of the people. There is no native culture in the cities. It is all foreign. It is all imported. It is not Venezuelan."

In an institute on a hill in the suburbs of the city the anthropologist has created an archive for the cultures she believes are vanishing. There are dozens of filing cabinets full of tape recordings and rituals and chants and photographs and ceremonials and sorcery and magic.

"Someone has to try to preserve the culture of the people if the people cannot," the anthropologist says to me. "That way, some day we can teach the people what they have forgotten."

"But, can you really preserve a culture in a filing cabinet?" I ask.

"Of course," she says. "Since we preserve it with scientific accuracy, you might say that in the filing cabinets it exists in its purest and truest form."

* * *

The light blue candles are burning in a line on the floor of the *barrio* home. All five candles burn with the same palest of lights. In the middle of the room cloves of garlic and medicine herbs are scattered in a circle around the feet of the sorcerer. She is an ordinary housewife sitting on her kitchen chair, her apron not quite concealing her slightly pregnant belly, and her little daughter clinging to her skirt. Suddenly she stands up. Her body stiffens. Her face becomes rigid.

In the swollen eyes of the woman there are no pupils. They have disappeared. Her eyeballs are white and empty as soft-boiled eggs without any yokes. The dark skin around her eyes seems blacker because of this. She is a sorcerer. In her trance she begins to moan an archaic African chant that has no words.

Deep down, in her sex, a quivering begins. It moves upward, through her body, until the staccato shivering has possessed her torso, her limbs, her neck, her head. But, her trance is neither violent nor hysterical; it quietly and warmly possesses her entire body. The black woman appears somewhat startled and uncomprehending about what has happened to her. Her body becomes very still. In her fear, she lifts the cross that hangs about her neck and kisses it, as she makes a sign of the cross as if to protect herself from herself.

At her knees, her daughter, who has seen her mother go into a trance before, begins to shiver and shake in imitation of her mother. The child's face seems to say: "Mothers all go into trances, don't they?"

The mother nudges the child away. And the little girl sits under the ironing board, in the laundry room of the *barrio* home, and sulks.

In the ceremony, the laundry room is transformed by the odors and spirits. So is the kitchen with its gleaming modern electric appliances. The living room where we sat waiting for the sorcerer to go into her ritual trance is just beyond the door. A splendidly middle-class room, it looks like the window of a furniture store. Of all the homes in this poorest of poor *barrios,* the sorcerer's may be, as it should be, the richest. But, the sorcerer has shut the door of the laundry room to the world beyond.

The black woman, her face becoming a death mask, begins to speak. Her voice is not her own. It is high-pitched and faint, as though it is coming from someone who is inside of her body. And the words are muffled.

"My spirit is the spirit of great Tamanaco," she says. "Yes. I am the spirit of *cacique* Tamanaco. And I have come to you, who are not an Indian, because there is the spirit of an Indian inside of you whom you do not know.

"Listen! I have come to teach you about your spirit," she says. She rises from the kitchen chair. Her hands outstretched, her eyes hollowed and blind, she walks across the room, barefoot, stepping over the burning candles, to where I am sitting. In front of me she stops. And her fingers reach out and grasp my head. The odor of rum and garlic pervades her body.

In her fingers' grip I feel that my skin contracts. My skull is compressed. She does not merely hold my head in her hands, but rather her fingers dig into my hair until they seem to have penetrated my skin and have entered into my brain.

And I instinctively seek to free my head. I do not know this woman. Nor does she know me. We have never met before. When somebody whom I do not know touches me intimately I always shy away from them. I do not like to be touched by strangers.

The woman's fingers are unrelenting. She will not let go. Her grip tightens, as though my brain was made of clay she wishes to mold.

"Listen! You have the spirit of an Indian," she says, "but you do not know who it is because you do not know its name. Maybe it does not want to tell you. Maybe you should not know. But, I feel it is a strong spirit," she says. "It is a very strong spirit. It has a powerful force. It has a steady force. The force is coming very stongly into my fingers. But, it will not tell me its name.

"But, when you go among the Indian people, they know it. That may be why they let you come to them. And that may be why they talk to you. But, in the past, there was a woman who would not let you follow the spirit. She stood in its way. She did not understand your spirit. Now she is gone from your way. Now you are free to become as strong as the spirit who is in you. But, you do not know how. You try to. But, you do not know the way.

"But, because of the spirit who is in you, you see things others do not see, you know things that you do not know, and you bring a good spirit with you and for that we thank you and protect you.

"You are a good white man, even if you are a white man. But, you are not completely a white man because the spirit in you is not a white man.

"But, sometime you will come with me to the mountain where we go. I, the *cacique* Tamanaco, here invite you to come to the mountain with me. Sometime, not this time, but when the spirit in you is ready, you will come to the mountain. But, now that is all I, the *cacique* Tamanaco, have to say."

The sorcerer walks backward over the burning candles. She sits down once more in the kitchen chair. Her body shivers and trembles. a sigh that sounds like a death rattle squeezes from between her lips with her spittle, and drips from her chin, and her limbs quiver and shake once more, and her face twitches and becomes still, and her dark pupils reappear in her white eyes. And she smiles.

My friend, the daughter of a former general, who has taken me to see the black sorcerer, warmly holds my hand

and says, "It is good." Her sister gathers up the black cloth bundle of hidden fetishes and sacred amulets that is lying on the floor in the circle of garlie cloves and medicine herbs. She blows out the candles.

In the living room of the suburban home of the black sorcerer we relax and drink coffee. Several overstuffed sofas and armchairs crowd the room. In the corner there is an upholstered bar. There are a pair of modern Swedish lighting fixtures hanging from the ceiling. On the coffee table there is the usual collection of bric-a-brac: two red ashtrays in the shape of baby's feet, the statue of a ceramic boy dressed in an eighteenth century costume, a green vase made of two praying hands, a horned African mask, and a gallon bottle of White Label Scotch.

As any gracious hostess would, the sorcerer serves her coffee in demitasse cups. We sit and sip and chat. The conversation is about the most mundane and commonplace things—the high prices in the supermarkets and the traffic jams on the superhighways of Caracas.

In time it is time to go. Politely, the black sorcerer of the *barrios* walks us to the door. And we embrace. "It has been so nice," she says, as though we had come for tea, and as we walk down her garden path to the Mercedes Benz she calls after us, pleasantly, "When you come back to Venezuela, you must come for another visit."

She waves goodbye. And her little girl waves too.

* * *

They live on the mountains above, beyond, and around the city. They live in *ranchos* like those they lived in, in the *campos.* They most often do not have electricity and running water and cooking gas and sewage pipes and paved streets. They do have television sets. They are not even urban peasants, but are merely *campesinos* living on the borders of the city. They have no passports. They are strangers even to themselves.

Some say that there are more than two million people in Caracas. Some say there are three million. Some say four. Some say less. Some say more. It does not matter. No one knows. No one can. No one ever will.

The people do not know themselves.

* * *

On a mountain slope, in one of the *ranchos* above the city, lives the family of Rafáel Montero. He is a leader of the *barrio.* Some men have good faces. He has such a face. Though he has just been awakened from an afternoon nap, his face is composed and friendly. And his white undershirt is clean and his hair is unruffled, even before strangers. Come and sit down, he says with his hands. "You are a guest in the poor house of a poor man," he boasts. And what kind of man is he?

"Ah, I am a peaceful man," he says. "I got married to learn tranquility and modesty."

His wife, cooking in the kitchen, hears the conversation and she comes into the room and wipes her hands on her dress and laughs. "Such nonsense!" she says. "If you talk such nonsense maybe you should see a psychiatrist."

The husband shrugs. "Who can ever please a woman," his expression says. But her face says, "He is no saint."

On the wall facing the door is a large framed portrait of Christ; He is standing in front of a clock whose hands indicate that is it five minutes to twelve and He is pointing an accusing finger at everyone who enters the house, in warning. Beside the portrait of Christ, on a shelf, there is a small television set, neatly covered with a lacy flowered cloth.

Señor Montero says that he built his house by himself, with his own hands. He is proud of it. Once he finishes his work for the post office he comes home, and works on his house. But, he says, he is too poor to do much.

The *rancho* and the two small bedrooms house the entire Montero family: the father and mother, and mother's mother, and four children. Still, it is larger than most *ranchos* in the *barrio,* and it is built better. Even so, the walls are dulled by mildew and the smells of poverty pervade it.

Behind the kitchen, with its wood stove, in the few feet between the hill and the back wall, there is an open sewage ditch that runs down the hillside. The wind is fortunately blowing in the other direction this morning.

On the edge of the sewage ditch the father keeps his cages of songbirds. They sing sweetly.

"God was good to us!" says Señor Montero. "The people in many *barrios* live much worse. For eighteen years we have lived here and we have worked hard with no help from anyone to make our house as good as we could. It has taken many years of sacrifice. But, what do we have?

"The walls of this house of ours are so thin they are falling down. And if there is a fire we lose everything. There is no water here. No protection. No police. No firemen. No green places for the children to play. No safety. No peace. No silence.

"So we formed a Committee of the *Barrios* and we went to the authorities and we asked them to help us to improve our conditions. But they said no. They could do nothing. And that is what they did. Nothing.

"And so the Communists come to us, these people who say they are from the Left and who have the passion for the poor. But they give us no solution to the fighting among the people; for a marriage of the people. The Communists think that everything is politics. And politics can solve everything. But all they offer is more fighting. Even so, I hear people say that we are Communists because we want a better life. That is because the people who say that already have a better life."

It amused him. So many people always came to the *barrio* and said that they wanted to help the poor when they really wanted to help themselves. They succeeded more in the latter, he thought, than in the former.

"These things make the people become discouraged. And they become conformists. You know Venezuelan men love rum and games; they love everything as they love a woman; they love dominoes and *boletas* and horse racing and lotteries as they love a woman—for the fun of it. And they love to argue without having a solution to the argument and without having to do anything.

"I am not like that. I have four cans of beer a week. As Abraham Lincoln said: 'One must always do good things and then the bad things will go away.' Maybe that is all a simple man can do."

There was no coffee in the house for guests. But formality decreed that something be served. His wife brought us a glass of water.

Of all the things in the *barrio* the one that insulted him the most was not the indignity of poverty, he said. If he wished he could be comforted by the obscurity of the *barrio,* for misery offered a man a hiding place. No! What insulted him was the helplessness that he felt when he tried to be a good citizen and do something.

"Our government should have a campaign of social sensibility. The people should be allowed to participate in the democracy. Many people in the *ranchos* do love their country, but they are not permitted to do anything to make their lives better. If they could, then we would be a great country. But the government does not come knocking on my door like the *evangelistas* do.

"For myself? What can one man do by himself? After I retire from the post office I will go to live in the countryside, in the interior. To a clean river. To the trees. To be with men who like to work hard, as we did in the old days. To a good life.

"In the countryside the people do live better than in Caracas. The poorest *campesino* has purer air to breath. He has more oxygen, more food he can grow, and he has more peace in his mind. Many people in the *ranchos* think that way, but they have no money to move. So they stay here until they die. For myself, I will go!"

Now he beckons us to come with him. "Come with me," he says, "and I will show you my cages of songbirds. They are happy. They do not know that they are singing beside a sewage ditch. So they go on singing."

"Listen," he says, proudly. "Do you hear them singing?"

* * *

The market stalls line the alley behind the old market. In the midst of the crowd of shoppers a crippled woman drags her body along the pavement. She swings her twisted legs in front of her and pulls her torso after them, balancing herself on a wooden block she holds in her hand. Her movements have a sort of grotesque grace, a poetry of pain, a tortured beauty. And yet, she is not a freak, she is not ugly, she is not old. She is simply crippled.

And she walks with speed and dexterity, on her hands. Her body moves in and out of the legs of the men, faster than they can.

By the entrance to the old market a blind man sits with a little boy on his lap. The boy begs in a small voice, but the blind man is more interested in the approach of the crippled woman whose body, slithering along the pavement, he recognizes by the sound it makes. Soon as the woman reaches the blind man they exchange a touch of recognition with their fingertips. He gives her a few coins. She pockets them.

And she drags herself away, without a word, through the crowds of shoppers, her legs in front of her, pulling her torso after them. She swings her body inch by inch over the pavement as if she is a crippled insect.

The blind man smiles contentedly and the little boy goes on begging.

On the plaza, down the street, three young boys are riding their skateboards. They are wearing polo shirts printed with the words, "The New York Times," and "The Los Angeles Dodgers," and "I Am Number One, Why Try Harder?"

* * *

"The seven wonders of the world. If we were to build them in Caracas, the *ranchos,* the slums, where millions of the poor live, would overshadow them," says Dr. Nelson Vásquez, director of the Maraven oil fields on Lake

Maracaibo. "Caracas is a magnificent city! We *Caracqueños,* and I am a *Caracqueño,* are very proud of our city. But, the truth is, if we were to build the seven wonders of the world and looked up and saw the *ranchos,* we would know that we were still in hell."

"No, no! Caracas is not quite as bad as that," says Claude Brun, the city planner of Guayana. "The truth is that Caracas is not hell! It is merely purgatory! Always in the countryside the people used to call Caracas the 'City of Purgatory'," Brun says. "Now they say, of course, the *Caracqueños* have the best of everything. But, I think the people in Caracas know that is not so. They know they are suffering from all the plagues of Egypt.

"But, after all, purgatory is better," Brun smiles, "than hell."

Of God

Where once Jesus Christ was crucified upon His sacrificial cross there is now a statue of Simón Bolívar. There is no altar in the church. There are no pews. In the church of Santa Trinidad, on a high hill in Caracas there is now a pantheon, as it is called, for the worship and adoration of the Liberator. And where the altar once stood there now stands the massive marble coffin of Bolívar, the father of the Republic, the son of the people, the holy ghost of unfulfilled aspirations and lost visions.

A young woman from Caracas who is visiting the tomb with me whispers: "Tell me, do you think that there are worms in Bolívar's coffin?"

"Dust," I reply.

She is silenced. The thought that a great hero may turn to dust is suddenly overwhelming to her.

On either side of the nave of the church, where the

statues of Mary and Joseph once may have stood, are the open crypts of Generals Sucre and Miranda. These heros of the wars of independence are not in their coffins. Sucre's body is in Ecuador, where that government refuses to permit its return to his native land, and Miranda's body has never been found. And so, the lids on the crypts of these heroes are kept ajar.

The shrine consists of this. Nothing more; for it is Bolívar and Bolívar alone who is worshipped here.

In all the country towns on the *campos,* no matter how small, there is the statue of Bolívar. The *barrios* of each city, no matter how poor, have their own Plaza Bolívar where the wreaths of homage never cease, day after day, for any and all celebrations and joyous occasions, times of mourning, and memories of sorrows. He is the saint of the people, celebrated as all saints should be, for what he suffered as much as for what he achieved, for not only his successes, but also for his defeats.

His coffin is its own altar. His corpse has crossed the mountains to its resting place. His body lies not in, but above the earth. Where the crucifixion was, in the church, he has taken the place of Jesus Christ.

By my side the young woman whispers incredulously, "Do you really think he is only dust?"

* * *

One of the calmest and oldest cities in the country is Cumana. Its quiet has the patina of centuries. And it is a fitting residence for His Excellence, Mariano José Parra León, the aged Bishop of Cumaná, who is said to be a deeply meditative man. I do not know him. However, my friend, Archbishop Roberto Sanchez of New Mexico, who does, has given me an introduction. "You must see him," he says to me, and though I try to see him the Bishop of Cumaná fortunately does not answer his telephone. If he had, I would be dead.

The old Bishop is not a recluse. But he does not get about much anymore. He is in his eighties and the journey to the capital is strenuous. So, if I wish to talk to him I will have to go to him, to his bedside if necessary.

My wish is to talk with him not about the church, but about its "soul." Where is the "soul" of the church? That is the sort of thing you can only ask an old man and only an old man can answer, if merely to say to you: "There is no answer."

For a week, every day, a telephone call is placed to the Bishop's residence in Cumaná. There is no answer. Perhaps he is ill, I tell myself. Or perhaps he is in a retreat. In disappointment I cancel my flight to Cumaná and I return my airplane ticket.

Black headlines in the morning's newspaper proclaim: "No Survivors!"

The flight has crashed into the Caribbean. It has sunk into deep water. Everybody is dead. On the flight's manifest they list forty-three passengers, and four in the crew, forty-seven dead, minus one—me.

I remember the Spirit Woman, who in her Afro-Indian rituals had told me a few days before not to seek to know too many things that no one could know. That is a dangerous path, she had said; do not go that way.

So, I do not try to see the Bishop of Cumaná. Instead, some days later, I pay a visit to the Bishop of Caracas, R. Ovidio Pérez Morales, who is General Secretary of the

Catholic Church Conference of Venezuela. His office in downtown Caracas is not only nearer but is quite a bit safer.

Even so, the commercial center of the city seems to be an unlikely place to seek the soul of anything. But why? The pulse of the country emanates from these office buildings of downtown Caracas; why not its soul? The office of the Bishop is properly like that of a lawyer.

"And how can I help you?" Bishop Pérez says.

"Where is the soul of Venezuela?" I say to him.

"The soul?" The Bishop falters. "Did you say the soul?"

"Yes," I say. "I am looking for the soul of Venezuela. And I cannot find it anywhere. Is it in the church?"

Bishop Pérez is a pragmatic man of vision they say. In effect, he is administrator of the church's affairs and he balances the ecclesiastical accounts. His logic is reasoning and his voice is reasonable but firm. And he judiciously weighs my words for any measure of falseness.

"The soul?" nods the Bishop. And his expression, bemused by my presumption, seems to say: "Is that all you are seeking? Nothing more?"

"Yes," I say weakly.

"If you wish to know the soul, you must know the body," the Bishop says. and he sets forth to instruct me with a talk that becomes a lecture and a lecture that becomes a treatise.

The Bishop says: "Now, we have gone crazy with material things. We are crazy. There are so many things we think we want and so many things we do not need, that the abundance of material things has become dehumanizing. And the spiritual life of the people has been thwarted. It is not good for people to be too poor, and it is not good for people to be too rich. But, I think the abundance of petroleum dollars has increased the social differences among the people. The circle of privilege and the circle of poverty have become larger. The abundance of money means that some people have the privileges of Europe, apartments in Miami, and castles in Switzerland. And some people have only little huts in the slums, the *ranchos*.

"Some of the people are so happy with their material things that they manage the country in a superficial manner. There has been a deterioration of ethical conduct and moral attitudes in these last few years. An increase in corruption is taking place, not only in the government, but in ordinary life. There is an attitude to acquire money, in any way they can.

"Money, money, money. So much of all we have has come from the petroleum dollars that I fear what may happen if the situation changes, if the petroleum stops.

"The democracy that we have here is a very delicate flower. A flower we must care for and look after. If we do not, the military might have the temptation of making a coup d'etat. There are people who say we have too much democracy. There are people who say our moral deterioration is due to this democracy and we need a firmer control. And so, it is necessary for us to protect our delicate flower. The abundance we have may lead to the destruction of the democracy that has helped create it.

"So, you see, the soul of Venezuela is in trouble. The church is concerned about these things. For hundreds of years we were the third rate colony of Spain. The Spaniards did not trouble themselves much about us because we were poor compared to Peru and Mexico. And that was good and bad. In our country it was easier for foreigners from all over Europe to settle. So our people have become very mixed. They are open to new people, to new ideas. They are not prejudiced against people of other countries. And we are not nationalists in the sense of being closed to strangers. We had a democracy of poverty.

"There is a democratic spirit in our country that is very old. It is not an accident that we are a democracy. But, the church was not as strong in our country as it was in Peru and Mexico. From the beginning of our independence, in 1830, there was a clash between the church and the governments. In the nineteenth century the Bishops were expelled. The Catholic schools and religious orders were abolished. Here, it was the conservative party that had ordered these measures against the church. Not the liberals. It was a peculiarity of politics that existed only in Venezuela and nowhere else in South America.

"So, because of our church history there is a more liberal spirit, I think, in our church. When the Catholic groups began to form in the universities under the democracy, they were not conservative. They were founded in the spirit of Catholic Action, and the majority of the students in the Catholic universities had a leftist leadership.

"I am not saying that the church was without sin. Some in the church did support the dictatorships, not because they agreed with them, but because they wanted peace. But, there were many in the church who supported the democracy, and the democratic revolutionaries.

"Now, we in the church believe in the plurality of political parties. We have learned the inconveniences caused by the interference of the church in politics. We feel it is better for the church to offer its ideas in politics, but to stay out of politics.

"Personally, I think it is not a good thing for the church to have political power. Of course, the position of the church depends on its leaders in a given moment in history and on the conditions that exist. These conditions, in Venezuela, are not created by those who lead the church.

"We live in a democracy. Like the fish lives in the water. And we talk of Christianity and democracy in ways that are easily understood in our country. It is not the same in some other countries in South America. The church there, if it said the things we say here, would be persecuted.

"There is a greater acceptance of many things here, for example, in the case of divorce. In Venezuela divorce was introduced many decades ago. That does not mean we in the church look upon divorce with favor. Rather it means that we recognize that divorce exists. In our pastoral letter on divorce we wrote that, of course, divorce is not good, but we in the church had to develop a pastoral relationship with people who are divorced, so they will know that they have not been abandoned by God.

"And the same is true with popular manifestations of religiosity. The popular forms of religion have to be respected. It is true that some of the popular religious practices sometimes seem like the worship of idols. But, one has to look closer.

"Some of the Catholic practice of the people is not so pure. There is some contamination by mysticism and superstition. But, in the villages, the Catholic faith has been continued year after year, often without priests, by people who have taken the name of teacher, or by families themselves, and that has to be respected, and honored.

"Even among the Marxists there are those who see things with a Catholic consciousness. They talk of Marxism as not incompatible with Christianity and Catholicism. A few years ago that would have been unheard of.

"These things give me hope in the future, in our future. Catholicism may die in our country. It is possible. It may become corrupted. Remember what has happened to the church in North Africa and in Turkey and in other places. But, I am a theological optimist. I believe there will be a new spiritual rejuvenation, a revival. In the church we are preparing for this by making the participation of the people greater in parish life. The women are becoming leaders in our religious communities. And that is something new, something very new, here in Venezuela. We are creating more Venezuelan ways of doing things in the church in our country.

"That, you may say, is because we do have faith in the Venezuelan soul. So you see I do not believe that it is true that we have lost our soul. Although, we may lose it."

Bishop Pérez has not paused once through his talk. He now seems tired and satisfied. Though he does not say so, his manner says: "Does that answer your unanswerable question?"

In leaving, I seek to thank him for being catholic as well as Catholic. But, he frowns, not understanding my poor compliment. So, I tell him that someone had told me he was a pragmatist, and I am delighted that he spoke so deeply of moral matters.

"Are there any others?" he asks.

On coming home, I tell Archbishop Sanchez of my meeting with Bishop Pérez. And I tell him, as well, why I did not see his friend, the Bishop Parra of Cumaná, of my quest for the Venezuelan soul, of the airplane flight that had crashed into the Caribbean, of the dead passengers, of my empty seat on the plane.

"Thank God," says the Archbishop, "some people are too busy to answer the telephone."

* * *

Inside the gutted cathedral there is the statue of the Virgin. She huddles under the filthy tarpaulin which protects her from the plaster that falls like rain from the ceiling, and she cowers there, the poor wife of a *campesino* huddling under her muddy *sarape.* No one cares. The communion rail has been torn from the floor before the altar and it lies outside the cathedral in the dirt. So do the stained-glass windows that once illuminated the mass with the heavenly glow of the sun and the moon; the scene of the resurrection is streaked with mud.

The face of Christ is missing in one of the stained-glass windows. Where His head had been there is a hole. His halo is gone, too. And yet, the desecration is not the work of atheists. Nor of revolutionaries. Nor of thieves.

Upon the hill of the old capitol of Ciudad Bolívar, across the plaza from the building where the constitution of the Republic was signed, the government has decided to restore the cathedral to its former glory, which it never had. It is doing so to honor the new spirit of independence that has come from the petroleum riches. And so the pews, the altar, the stained glass windows, the communion rail, and the face of Christ have all been removed. They will evidently be modernized. In the meantime, the cathedral stands empty, an unfinished construction project waiting for the advent of its coming glory.

In the mud near the communion rail, one of the workmen has left an empty beer can. Standing beside the stained glass windows I can see the beer can in the hole where the head of Christ had once been.

And Love

On the grass the young lovers lie entwined like lily pods on the still waters of a pond. And they are all like the same flower, for each couple is lying in the same position. The boy sits and the girl lies beside him, her body bent backward, her face upward, in his lap. In this way the boy can lean forward and enclose the girl in his arms, so she is entwined as any flower, by the flower of her lover. She seems to be drinking his kisses from his lips.

The young lovers in the park lie like this for hours, for days, for months, for years. If they can. One afternoon as I walk through the *Parque de Los Caobos*, in Caracas, I see dozens of young lovers lying in exactly this way. And that evening, when I walk through the park again, maybe three hours later, they do not seem to have moved a finger.

Sometimes they are so entwined it is not possible to see where the boy begins and the girl ends. They seem to be one being. Even so, in the evening the young lovers must rise from the beds of grass. It is time to separate. The breeze from the *autopista* of Francisco Fajardo comes from the rush of traffic and there is a rustling in the leaves of the palm trees and the blouses of the young girls. One by one, or two by two, the lovers begin to emerge from their entwined limbs and wander off, arm-in-arm, holding tightly onto each other's bodies, as though they do not wish to separate and become divided by society's definitions of men and women. But, they have no choice.

For the truth is that these young lovers have not come to the park to make love to one another. Nor have they come to escape from the city; that is impossible. They have come to lie in peace in each other's arms, as far away as they can be from the demands that govern the love of men and women, the bravado of *machismo* and the codes of virginity. In the park the men do not have to pretend to be *macho.* And the women do not have to pretend a coquettish innocence. Here, in the park, they may be simply lovers and equals.

* * *

In a cafe, while we are having our lunch, my companion begins to instruct me in the moralities of loving. He is an engineer, recently graduated from the university. So, though he speaks articulately of the moralities and necessities that govern the behavior of men and women, there is a wry and rueful look on his face all the while, as though he knows that he is voicing a paradox.

"Love," he says, "is never a crime in our country the way

it is up in your country. Nor is sex. That may be why *macho* is important for men, and virginity for women," he says. "Maybe because we are freer in love we place a higher value on a man being a man and a girl a virgin."

I thought at first that he was being sardonic. But, he is not.

"If a girl says she is a virgin before she gets married and she is lying, she will be in serious trouble," he says. "Most especially if her husband is not the man who did it. He doesn't want any girl who isn't a virgin. He wants to be the first with her."

And trying to understand this, I ask: "But, the man, he doesn't have to be a virgin, does he?"

"No," he says seriously. "The man, of course, doesn't have to be a virgin. It is impossible for a man. But, for a girl it is a different matter."

"How can that be?" I ask.

Now my friend begins to sense I am not as sympathetic as I seem. "If the man is not a virgin then there must be a woman who is not a virgin, as well," I say. "Who do men go to?"

"Men go to whores for that. And divorced women," he replies. "The whorehouses are legal. And the woman who is divorced is going to have a hard time, anyway, finding a husband. She knows that most men will not marry her. If she is a professional woman, even a secretary, it may be easier for her, but if she is just an ordinary housewife or a country woman, then it isn't going to be easy for her to find a man to marry."

"Sometimes when a girl has a baby in a town in the *campos,* she will have to leave the town. And she has to go to the city," he shrugs. "No man will marry her if he knows."

"But, they will sleep with her," I say. "Even more so?"

"Ah yes," he laughs. "The lack of virginity does not hurt in the making of love. It is the morality that is important, you see."

* * *

One young woman says: "Men are like children here. They all want a woman who will take care of them. Like a child who is at its mother's breasts, they want to be loved all the time. It is so boring. There are so many exciting things to do besides making love all the time. There is the discussion of things, learning things, becoming friends. But, the men do not want to be a woman's friend. All they want to do is make love. How boring! I like to talk to a man. Making love gives me a headache."

One young man says: "Sometimes in the streets when I see a woman's ass, I go blind. I cannot see anything else. I don't look at her face. That is my weakness. And I like a woman's ass to be the right size—small. You know, something that you can get your hands on and hold in your hands without any trouble. Small enough so that she fits in the palms of your hands, so to speak. Most men I know are like this. They don't judge a woman by looking at her face. It is her ass that is really important."

One young woman says: "For a year and a half I was living with a man. We were lovers. That is, he said he loved me, but he didn't. Sometimes I think he really hated me. Twice when I got a job he made me quit. 'Come here, you belong with me,' he would shout. And I would come. I loved him and so I thought I could make him treat me with love. But, I couldn't. One day I said; 'That's it!' And I left him. I am learning how to be independent. For a Venezuelan woman that isn't easy. Now, sometimes I am lonely and I think it would be nice to have a man, a man who would protect me and who would make me feel secure, by being not only my lover but my friend. And then, I think, where is there any man like that?"

One young man says: "Men consider a woman to be a sex machine. It is true of most men in this country. They do not want to have a woman as a friend, as a companion, as someone they can talk to about serious things. A woman is just for sex. And so, the women respond to that. They lie there like wooden boards. They will not touch a man when they make love because they feel that sex is something for the man to do to them. They feel sex is dirty.

"Once when I was going with a woman and it came time, she got undressed and lay down on the bed as if she were asleep. I said to her: 'Are you dead? Why don't you act alive?' But she could not. She tried, but she was too embarrassed. And so, I said to her: 'Let's get dressed and go dancing.' In dancing, at least, she acted as if she were interested and enjoying herself."

One young woman says: "There is a story of the two men, two friends who were doctors in Caracas, and who went on a vacation together, to the Andes, with their mistresses. Maybe their secretaries. Not their wives, just their mistresses. In a bar one of these mistresses was, how do you say, 'showing off' what she had. And the other man, he was a little drunk, he was admiring her. So his friend took out a gun and shot him dead.

"And that is how men feel about their women. They think they own them. They behave as if the women were part of their own bodies, the bodies of the men."

One young man says: "The women are the hobby of the men in this country. Men do not think of women as people, but as toys that they play with. One reason is that it is very hard to have a woman. It takes so long. So, having a woman becomes the hobby of men, like a game they play, but they know they will not often win. That is why men spend all their lives playing the game. The women play the game too. Maybe the women like being the hobbies of the men. They complain, but they play the game anyway."

One young woman says: "Once a woman belongs to a man she always belongs to him until he decides to leave her. That's how the men think. So a woman learns to be cautious. Even now, my mother will not go out of their house without my father. That's how she feels. He can go out anytime, anywhere he wishes to. But she will not. If she did, God knows what he would do. She is afraid of that."

One young man says: "Most of the women in our country have a virginity of the mind. It is worse than virginity of the body. The virginity of the body can be changed. But, the virginity of the mind? Never! Never! And most of the men, they have virginity of the mind, too. Though with the men it is in the form of *macho.* Like the women, most of these men think of making love as something dirty and sinful. But, to the men, that makes it more exciting. So, you see, these men have virginity of the mind, too."

One young woman says: "All the men in this country

think they are *macho*. I never met a man who did not think that way. In the university, the men are as *macho* as the men in the *barrio*. They may believe in all sorts of radical theories and they may be socialists, they may even be Marxists, but when it comes to women's rights they are as *macho* as everybody else. They feel it is their right to ask a woman to go to bed with them whenever and wherever they wish. They feel threatened by talk of women's rights. They feel it is the right of a man to do certain things, but it is not the right of a woman. And they are right, of course. Men can do and say things that a woman is not permitted to say or do.

"And men are very strange about it because it hurts them as much as it does the women. But, they don't see it that way. They are blind."

* * *

On a cool evening under the palm trees in an open air restaurant by the beach of Porto de la Cruz I sit sipping beer and watching the young girls stroll in the twilight. The lovely sight inspires a young man beside me to sigh wistfully and comment on the comparative anthropology of love. He tells me a folktale of the ways of love, if not loving. He says it is a national joke which men tell one another in the country. But he does not laugh.

This is what he says: "After you make love to an American woman, she says, 'Give me a cigarette.'

"After you make love to an Italian woman, she says, 'Give me some more.'

"After you make love to a French woman, she says, 'Oh, what a pity there were not three of us.'

"After you make love to an English woman, she says, 'My dear, what did you say your name was?'

"After you make love to an Argentinian woman, she says, 'Let me introduce you to my family.'

"After you make love to a Brazilian woman, she says, 'Let me introduce you to my husband.'

"After you make love to a Chinese woman, she says nothing.

"But, after you make love to a Venezuelan woman, she says, 'My God, what will people think of me?'"

* * *

A delicate summer dress of sheer silk decorated with pastel flowers so translucent that they appear to be spun from the gossamer wings of butterflies. On her neck wind three long strands of the whitest pearls, perfectly matched. She wears these adornments of her femininity with a dignity that seems all the more regal because it is so remarkably casual. In her gracious and genteel way she is a vivacious woman, sometimes fervent in her beliefs, but always properly ladylike.

Ladylike is the word that best describes her, to me, though the word seems peculiarly apolitical. Dr. Ana Lucina Garcia Maldonado is president of *La Federación Venezolana de Abogadas,* the Federation of Women Lawyers, one of the most powerful women's groups in the country. She, on this day of our meeting, is chairing a session of the International Congress of Women Lawyers in the great Hall of Nations. The meeting's purpose is nothing less than the rewriting of the laws in the Napoleonic Codes that govern the rights of women. And men. Nonetheless, there is an informality in her manner in spite of the dozens of delegates and officials who flutter around her with endless demands which she fulfills. She has a delighted laugh, as floral as her dress, that seems to take her by surprise as we talk. It certainly does me. Perhaps it is improper for me to be so charmed by a feminist leader.

"May I meet one of the leaders of the women's rights movement?" I had asked. "Someone who can articulate the contemporary problems of women, from a strongly feminist viewpoint, and yet can do so in a Venezuelan way." And she was recommended as that woman.

She is one of "our strongest and most articulate of feminists," I am told. And that turns out to be a considerable understatement.

This is what she tells me: "For women there is no mystique in *machismo*. It is a practical matter. It means that one of every five children is born out of wedlock. And the women have to raise them. To that you have to add the 60 percent of the children who are left with the woman after a couple separates and the man leaves. So for 80 percent of the children the woman is solely responsible. She looks after them, she feeds them, she raises them, she is the mother and father. That is *machismo!*

"Many men prefer to lose their jobs and go away, rather than pay anything for the upkeep of their children. They run away to another woman. So we are demanding a law that says men are financially responsible for their children.

"In our country, the men of *Criollo,* the *Mestizos,* have *machismo* in their heads. They feel they are the "*machos* of *machos!*" And to a man who feels this way, the woman is just a *cosa*—a thing, an object for his pleasure. These men do not even treat the woman as a housewife. A woman is merely a *cosa,* a thing, with whom the man can enjoy himself. And so, if a child is born of the man's enjoyment it is not the man's child, it is the woman's.

"And so, the woman is not permitted to do anything. She must stay home and be available for the man's enjoyment. That is *machismo!*

"Such a man feels his *machismo* depends on his being the master of the woman. He has to be the *cacique,* the chief. He has to have the legal right to decide everything. He has to earn the money. If the woman works then he may feel that he has lost his status as the *cacique.*

"Men feel free to have many children by different women because of this. The women, too, may have children by many men. So, there is no single father in the family. The family, most families, therefore, are headed by the women. It is not uncommon for a woman to have six or seven children, all of them by different men. And so, the woman has to be the head of the family; she holds the family together. Because of this, with no father in the home, our families tend to become matriarchies, ruled by women. That is *machismo!*

"And so, I think that *machismo* comes not from a man's strength, but comes from his weakness. It is a man's way of running away from his responsibilities. He leaves the woman to do the 'man's job'. He confers fatherhood on her. It is a paradox. But, the *machismo* of men is really a sign of how weak men really are.

"Even so, *machismo* is an obstacle to the rights of women. There are many roads women cannot take. So, though women have political rights in our country, they do not have the civil rights to do what they have the political rights, on paper, to do. We have very few 'legal' rights. The rights of women are legally dated from the time of the Codes of Napoleon. In that time the woman had very few familial rights. Napoleon, like other men of that day, wanted only one thing from a woman. So, the Napoleonic Codes are concerned only with the rights for the men, not the women.

"Now, when a man and woman come to the city it is the man who has the right to decide where to build his house, their *rancho.* It is his. And if the man wants to get divorced, all that he has to do is go back to their village and get divorced, and his woman, in Caracas, may not know anything about it. The man can get a divorce simply by accusing his wife of adultery. He merely has to accuse her. He doesn't have to prove anything. But, the woman, if she wants a divorce, cannot accuse her husband of adultery. She has to prove it. That is *machismo!*

"And, if they separate, the man has the right to sell everything he wishes and keep the money. He doesn't have to give his wife and children anything. In Venezuela there is no law of common property. So the woman and children may be left with nothing.

"Even worse, if a man comes home and sees his wife in bed making love to another man, he may kill her, and the maximum he will be sentenced to is three years in jail. But, if a woman comes home and finds her husband in bed making love with another woman, and she kills him, she will face a charge of murder. She may be sentenced to thirty years in jail. That, too, is *machismo!*

"So, we wish to end these Napoleonic Codes. There should be equal rights for men and women. One of those laws in the Napoleonic Codes says that a woman need not appear in court. A woman may be excused simply because she is a woman. But the paradoxical thing about that is that 40 percent of the lawyers in our country are women!

"These things have to change. We want what you call 'human rights.' Forty years ago the women began to enter our national life, to enter the universities, to have a role in the development of the nation. Now, the women are everywhere. In the government 45 percent of the administrators are now women.

"There is a change in women that men have a difficulty in accepting. It is easier for a woman to change than it is for a man. I don't know why. But it is so. Men would like women to be just as they were in the old days; to be as quiet and obedient. But, the women have a different place in society now; they can go out of the house and get a job, and they are different women. So, the men are confused and angered by this. They don't understand. I think this is why there are so many divorces these days.

"Nowadays, the women will look for something new in a man. They are tired of the old *machismo.* They are tired of being taken advantage of by a man. Many of the young women wish to be themselves. They no longer wish to be a *cosa,* a thing for a man's enjoyment. So, these young women are looking for a man who will not try to place them in a house and make them stay there for their own pleasures. They wish a man who will be able to help them be themselves—not a man who will fight against them, but a man who will come with them, by their side.

"No, I am not optimistic. But I am realistic. One of the greatest revolutions of our time is the women's revolution. Latin America will never be the same again. I am looking forward to the day when there will be a woman who becomes President of this country. Not because she is a woman, but because it is the normal thing."

In the great Hall of Nations the International Congress of Women Lawyers is about to begin. There are many hundreds of women in the audience. And one man. Myself. "Come, be my guest," Dr. Ana Lucina Garcia Maldonado has said.

Bouquets of bright tropical flowers have turned the dais into a colorful garden. It is International Women's Day. This morning the leaders of the Congress had gone to the tomb of the Liberator, Simón Bolívar, and had laid a wreath at his feet as though seeking his blessing for their campaign for women's rights, in his land of *machismo*.

"Isn't there some irony in this?" I ask one of the feminist lawyers. Bolívar is the symbol of *machismo* in the country. His statue stands, with sword drawn, in every plaza. Old men revere him and little boys are taught to emulate him. "Surely, the man of *machismo* shall fight against you," I say.

"Not at all," she says. "In his time the Liberator all but went into battles with his mistress by his side. She saved him many times. And so, it is merely justice to ask him to fight for our liberation, by our side.

* * *

On the promenade by the river the girls walk hand-in-hand. They come by twos and threes and fours and fives and sixes. All evening the girls walk together along the river, under the cool moon of the savannah, arms around one another's waists and shoulders, holding onto one another's necks and buttocks, touching, always touching one another, like sisters. More fondly than young lovers do these girls walk together in chaste embrace. They do so with gentle hands.

It is Saturday night. On the promenade the young mothers have come, as well, with their little children. The husbands have gone drinking so the young mothers walk together, and alone.

For generations the women of Ciudad Bolívar have

walked in this way of the Paseo on the banks of the Orinoco, in the cool evenings. There is not much else to do in the old and traditional city. Some have come to seek no more than the fresh breeze from the river. Some seem to seek much more, but in the provincial capital women do not speak of things which they may seek. They walk in whispers. They do not talk loudly.

The evening air from the savannah is like a warm body; it reaches out with moist fingers to caress the strolling women with a touch of loneliness and longing. In the muted walk of the women there is a certain sadness and there is a sense of sorrow in the quiet of their voices as they comfort one another. They are women without men.

A man who has been watching the girls and women walking, says in anger: "These women are afraid of men. So they walk alone. Do you know why they do that? They are looking for a husband. Not for a man. For a husband. They want to make a duck of man, as we say."

"Goddamn virgins," he says. "They need a good fucking." Still, the women go on walking along the river in the evening by themselves. They go hand-in-hand, not looking at the young men who sit on the wall by the river embankment. They walk together not merely for self-protection, but seeking the touch of tenderness and affection of their gentle hands. Are there no young men in Ciudad Bolívar with gentle hands?

* * *

She stands with her hands on her large hips. The black woman has come out of her mud hut by the roadside and poses in the doorway with an aloof posture. In a graceful movement of her hand she lifts her right breast from the bodice of her dress and, cupping her fingers about the rounded, dark flesh, she offers it to me with a benign smile. And I return her smile, but shake my head.

And she spits.

The Search for the Lost Souls

The magical world of Levy Rossell is underground. In a subway tunnel under the Avenue of the Liberator there was once a dim passage, smelling of urine and dirtied by graffiti. Now it is crowded with dreams; it is his theater. Where the steps led down into a dark hole under the street, the steps are seats, and there is a bright stage, rehearsal halls and workshops hung with giant puppets whose heads are made of brooms, a rogues' gallery of clowns, even a museum, and in a corner there is a seamstress who sits and sews the costume of a human-sized chicken.

And, in many ways, the theater, under the earth, is more colorful and brighter than those under the sun. That is to be expected in a city where everything has been turned upside down. In Caracas, where the skyscrapers rise higher every day, its most popular theater is underground? Why not! This stage is no more absurd than life on the city streets. And besides, the paradox appeals to Levy Rossell. Even the location of his theater seems appropriate; it is on the edge of the *Parque de Los Caobos,* the park of young lovers, with the Museum of Fine Art on its left and the Caracas Hilton on its right.

Here, in this hole under the city, Rossell has set about recreating life as he dreams it. The image that his theater brings to mind is that of Alice in Wonderland, an image he does not discourage. But, he seems less an innocently devilish Alice than a devilishly innocent Mad Hatter.

The curly hair and large eyes do give him a cherubic and mischievously childlike appearance. But he is deceptive. So are his plays. In their comedy, and they all have a touch of comedy, is the laughter of clowns, the illusion of laughter that Rossell himself dons when he talks, like the mask of a conjurer, a shaman, a magician.

And so I ask him: "Is it true, as they say, that you are a magician?"

He says: "No, the artists do not deal with magic. We are magic! We are not magicians! We are magic! I am magic! Let me tell you this about myself. When I really need something for my work, and I think about it, then it realizes itself. These are material things that I am talking about. Maybe I need a cow for the performance. And I can't find a cow in Caracas. And someone will call me and say; 'Listen, I have a cow for you!'

"That is what art is. It is magic. It makes things happen in life magically. And that is what I feel our art tells the people: 'Here is the power of magic, if you want it.'

And I say to him: "Do the people listen to your wise words?"

He says, "My?"

"Your wise words."

"My wise?"

"Your profound words."

"Ah, *mi profundo, mi palabra, profundo,* my profound words?"

"Yes."

"I have none," he says.

But, he is being less than honest with me. He is an outspoken man with an opinion about everything. And I am told the comic-tragic satire of his performances makes people think of a musical written by Gabriel García Marquez and Federico Fellini.

And I say to him: "I am searching for the Venezuelan soul. But, I have not found it. Maybe with your magic you can find it for me?"

He says: "So you are searching for the Venezuelan soul? Don't. You will never find it. It does not exist. There's a comfortable amnesia in our country. It is easier that way. Some people say that we Venezuelans seem like the gypsies of South America because we are always on the move. Because we have more than one face. Because we have many personalities. That's not true! That is demagogy! We have no personality at all. We have no identity. We have no face. We have lost it. We had an identity. But, we have been alienated from it. And we have been alienated from our own culture for a long time now.

"It is not real what has happened to us in Venezuela. It is no longer superficial. It is an apparition of life that seems to be alive because it lives on its own inner momentum, you know, but it is a 'singer without a song.'"

And I say to him: "What has happened to your identity?"

He says: "Here, the main problem is money. Too much money. Too much easy money. Everybody has the same opportunity to be a thief. Everybody is running in a great marathon to get all the money they can, in any way they can. Everybody is a thief so nobody is a thief.

"And you have to run. I am talking about myself, too. If you do not run in the marathon you have absolutely no possibility of surviving because a man is judged by his success, and his worth as a man is judged by his money.

"So, we have money, but no food. We have oil, but no water. We have wealth, but no culture. If culture is an 'imitation' of life, then the state of our culture tells you what is our life. The government imports culture as it does eggs and chickens and shoes and dresses. So, we consume the culture of other countries, though we could have had our own.

"Our culture of the past has been lost in the confusion of the times. And instead of our native culture we became passive buyers and consumers of foreign culture. So, our culture no longer will exist in our own country. And I fear what will happen when there is no more petroleum, no more money to buy culture. The people will have only their own thought and culture left, but they will have forgotten them. So all that we will have is a vacuum.

"Now we are a young and we are a rich and we are an uneducated land. And we need someone who shall say to us, as Jesus Christ said to Lazarus: 'And so you too shall fall!' Who will say that to us? Perhaps the future will. If the marathon continues, the time shall surely come to us, when we will have to fall."

And I say to him: "For a man who is famous for his comedy, for his gaiety, you have a tragic sense of happiness. I thought you were a romantic."

He says: "I believe in man. Was it Rousseau who said that man is good? Yes, man can be good, but in a bad society man is bad. To be good, man has to be free to be himself. So, I believe, man will change his ways, his characteristics. When that happens, he will become tired of this society. He will get tired of it."

And I say to him: "What will he tire of?"

He says: "Of being a shit! That will be a revelation. Man behaves contrary to his feelings. It is always so. In the works of every philosopher and artist you discover the same truth. Everyone wants to be beautiful, to be happy, to be good. Everyone has the same goal. That is a necessity for life. But, when a man enters society his behavior changes from his seeking this necessity of his life to that of fulfilling the necessity of the society. So, the task of the artist is to reawaken man to the necessity of his own life. To make it possible for him to be himself again.

"In the cycle of life we artists do not change man. No, we do not change anything. We reaffirm the cycle of life. Since we exist beyond time, we can cross the times of eternity and remind man he can begin again at the beginning of the cycle of his own life. That is why all new works of art are like the birth of a child. A new beginning. A newborn infant."

And I say to him: "Is that why you devote so much time to performing plays for children? For a nationally and internationally known theater to perform so many plays for children is very unusual. Why do you do it?"

He says: "I remember when I was in my mother's belly. Sensations. Thoughts. Feelings. These are things I remember in my mother's belly. And I can remember when I was one year old. When I was three or four, my thoughts became too much for me. And so I talked to myself. I had dialogues with myself. But, I remember that I had to stop thinking because my thoughts were too much for me.

"When I was five I came to Caracas because my parents were politically persecuted by the dictator, Jiménez. And so my father had to change his name and his appearance. That was a terrible time for me, as a child.

"I remember when I was a child I never knew beautiful things. Then I went to school and I learned about beautiful things. I remember my first time in singing class. I remember my teacher with a great love. I remember the first song I learned. Let me sing it for you.

> The autumn has to come.
> The autumn has to come.
> I will wait at my door.
> And autumn leaves fall.
> And they become golden.

"To be a child is to be alive to all of life. When you are the child you are not limited by time. As a child, the things you have stay alive in you. That is the importance of childhood, you know, that life stays alive in you in a much purer form, because when you are a child you are not limited by the necessities of society. As a child, you have the alternative, the option, the possibility of being good. I have a great respect for children. I love children.

"And so, we have plays for children in the *barrios*. From their hell we take them to heaven, a place we have in the mountains, our farm. There we play a play for them about how to take seeds, how to plant, how to grow plants, how to harvest. In the end we give the children seeds so they can plant them in the *ranchos* where they live. So our theater does not end with the end of our performance. It goes on, it grows, in their gardens.

"Once I had a dream. And my dream was that I was living in a city where all the trees were fruit trees. And instead of lawns and gardens there was every kind of vegetable for the poor people to eat. I told this dream to a city official and he told me that it was impossible to do in a city.

"But, in front of our theater we have a tree that is good only for shade. If it were a mango tree it would be just as full of shade, but would also give us food to eat. So many children in the streets have no food at all. It is not a fantasy to say we have hunger. No, I know children who have one cup of coffee for the whole day. In the city do you know how much we invest in our lawns and gardens? But, a hungry child cannot eat the grass and leaves.

"And so, we have made our theater into a garden for children. One critic has called me a grown-up child and an immature man. So I told him: 'I thank you. I appreciate the compliment.'"

There is a sign at the entrance of the theater that says, *Espectáculos Para Niños*: Spectacles for Children. It attracts as many fathers and mothers as sons and daughters.

On Sundays the plays for children begin. In the tunnel under the streets an actor appears upon the stage dressed in pink and green pantaloons, a red kerchief on his neck, wearing a too small, silver-spangled vest and a too large bow tie, a brown Andean hat on his head that is adorned with a great pink ribbon, and on his legs he has yellow and blue striped socks. He is, of course, the spirit of everyone's saint's day fiesta, black African dance, and Orinoco and Andean Indian ritual that has ever taken place in the country.

A little girl, in the front row, lets loose a red and white balloon on a string. It floats onto the stage where the actor adds it to his many costumes. He then begins to tell the story of *The Ugly Duckling*.

The stage becomes a stage for two puppet theaters, one large and one small, in which a Venezuelan Punch and Judy, the punchinellos of the *barrio,* begin to narrate a slide show, the puppeteers joining their puppets. Who are the marionettes and who are the masters? No one knows.

But, these children are not fooled. From their loud laughter and applause it is obvious that they know the people are the puppets and the actors are on strings.

So, when in the end the puppet of the ugly duckling turns into a polyfoam white swan, the children do not doubt it for a moment. They flap their arms like wings and fly away.

"You see! You see," exclaims Levy Rossell, "how all the little children fly away? They are freed."

* * *

For months I looked for a sign of the soul of the country. Then one day I found it. On the glass door of a gallery in the Museum of Fine Arts, in Caracas, is this sign:

Cerrado
Closed
Ferme
Chiuso
Geschlossen

The door, of course, was open.

In the Andes

On the flat lands of the Llanos the people say of the people in the high mountains: "They are devious! When they are poor and weak they will come to you on their knees and beg and bow and pretend to be humble. But, when they become rich and powerful they become tyrants! Most of our dictators and generals have come from the states of Táchira and Mérida in the Andes. They are never to be trusted!" And so they speak of the people of the high mountains as though they thought they were Indians.

And the people of the Andes will say of the people of the lowlands: "They have no principles!"

* * *

The face of the mountains beckons us. Not seductively, not enticingly, but with that stern countenance of a gaunt and stone goddess who is demanding and yet distant. There is something awesome about this embrace of the Andes, and it seems hopeless to resist the mountains when their towering arms reach down and pull you up to their cold breasts. From the tropical lowlands of the Llanos to the high passes, the road rises eleven thousand feet in a few miles. And we go with it, unwillingly.

Evening comes. In the evening in the mountains the darkness comes at once, instantly, without warning. As soon as the sun goes down beyond the highest ridge, the far sides of the mountains become cold and ominous. The road is lost in the mist; it vanishes into the darkness and is swallowed by the night.

The car's lights are cat's eyes in the gray mist. But, they cannot see into the abyss beneath the cliff on which the road clings as it winds and unwinds its way upwards, thousands of feet above the valley towards the Pass of the Mucuchies that straddles the gateway to the Andes at eleven thousand feet. Somehow the road seems suspended in the air.

On the serpentine road there are no guard rails. The mountain waterfalls splash across the road with a carefree sound. People have to share the passage with nature.

On the day that we ascended into the Andes there was a solar eclipse. It came just as we started upward, with the mountains to the right and the blinding light to the left. Before their bamboo huts the *campesinos* gathered and ignored the radio's warnings not to look at the sun, staring with wide open eyes. So did I.

When the sun melted into the moon, a strange thing happened. The Andes became white as ice and the dense tropical forests on the mountain slopes seemed to freeze as the leaves of the palm trees were illuminated from within, translucent as icicles. At that moment, the eternal snow on the peak of Mount Bolívar turned black, as black as rocks, as black as frozen petroleum, in the metamorphosis of the sun. It was as though everything was turned inside out.

That day, when we crossed the Andes in the blaze of light, was *El Dia de la Raza,* the Day of the Race, when the people of America were created according to an ancient legend. It is known, as well, by the cosmic-minded, as the day that a possibly Spanish, or Italian Jew who was named Colón sailed across the sea. That is, it is Columbus Day.

And so, the solar eclipse is celebrated in many ways by the people. The scientists study it, but these people of the villages in the Andes have for centuries revered the sun as the giver of life and the source of energy; the superstitious called this sun worship until they learned better. In any event, the road to the Pass of the Mucuchies is crowded on this day with people who stand by the roadside to be bathed, to be cleansed, to be expurgated by the fire in the sky. They wave to us as we go by.

Suddenly, at nine thousand feet, the road disappears. Lord, an avalanche of great rocks and tons of mud has fallen. It has buried half of the road. The remaining half of the road has fallen into oblivion, into the valley, leaving a jagged edge of cement. Our car rides over the crumbling rocks. There is no room to pass. And we do not pray; there is no time. It seems to me that two of our wheels are turning in midair as we swing around the debris, but that may merely be my fright. Either way, we go on. In an avalanche of mud and rock, if you turn back it may mean a wait of days.

Fortunately, I am not driving. My driver is an old hand

at crossing the Andes. He had come from the mountains of New Mexico to the mountains of Venezuela more than a decade ago, as a forestry man, and he has settled in Mérida, high in the Andean valleys, and has married a beautiful local woman from an old mountain family. Crossing the Andes from his work in the forests to his home in the mountains is like commuting, to him; he has done it hundreds of times.

Señor Vincent is the sort of man who was born in the wrong century. He knows how to talk to a tree and outwit a burro. And he drives as if our secondhand Dodge is four-footed. Surely it is more interesting to cross the Andes in the twilight, as he likes to, when the fog has descended and no more than a few feet of what's left of the road is visible. But why, if he must talk when he drives, must he talk with both of his hands so that he touches the steering wheel only infrequently, and by chance.

"You only live once," I say.

"And you only die once," my Venezuelan companion laughs.

"Even so," I say, "why not keep at least one hand on the wheel?"

"Of course," he says.

The facing of death on this mountain road is not really a challenge, for there is not much real threat. It might be a glorious death, a heroic death, to be hurled from a cliff in the Andes into the valley, like a sacrificial virgin wearing a modern suit of armor, our bright orange Dodge of ancient vintage and rusting chrome taking flight as if it's sprouted the wings of Icarus, to become a saint of the automotive age. Sadly, there is no hope of canonization for us. The statistics show fewer deaths on mountain roads than there are on the streets of a city.

Once, not too long ago, these mountain roads were burro trails. They have been paved and widened, but they have not changed too much. They are essentially still trails built for burros. And their ascent to heaven is a penance that must be suffered with faith.

For centuries, seekers and visionaries journeyed devotedly onto the Pass of the Mucuchies, searching for the mysteries that may be hidden beneath the shadows of the Andes. The noble Incas built their once-sacred cities to the sun, not far to the south. And here, the monks of Spain came to be close as they could to their gods. So, too, Simón Bolívar and his armies came this way on their quest for that illusory Republic of Gran Colombia, the Shangri-la of democracy that the hero of Venezuela's War for Independence wished to create with the Andes as its rocky spine. Bolívar, in his day, rode into the mountains over the Pass of the Mucuchies, on this very trail. He nearly died in doing so, as so many have done. And yet, in some way it was necessary for him, as for the rest, to cross the Andes to sanctify the holiness of their quest.

Of the many who have come this way, who is to say why they did not chose an easier path? No one, until our time, has ever conquered a mountain. And the men and women who climbed the Andes did not conquer them. They became part of them. In these mountains there is a strength that humans do not have.

On the Pass of the Mucuchies the wind blows the night into our faces. It is a cold and unrelenting force that freezes our eyes. And we seek shelter in a cafe in the pass, where tiny cups of dark coffee, black and sweet, warm our bones. In a corner is a dormant, neon-illuminated jukebox that rests in the shadows. The Beatles song in the machinery is silent. On the shelves are polo shirts and ash trays for the tourists: "Our Visit To The Andes." An old man greets my friends; they worked together in the forests, years ago.

Someone says: "It feels like snow."

"In the summer in the tropics?" I protest. They laugh.

The rain has begun. It is cold as snow. Soon it may freeze. And so we go on down into the valley of the Andes. On the sides of the road are old stone walls. Some of these are hundreds of years old. In ancient days the Andean Indians used the stones to terrace the mountains' slopes, so they could be farmed; the walls did not divide their land as much as they held it from being washed away in the avalanches of earth which came with each rainy season. Even now these stone walls seem to keep the land in rather than the people out; the land is the land of the family who farms it, but they do not own it. It belongs to the mountains. So do they.

Along the old burro trails which now are paved not with stones, but cement, the villages of the Andean Indians still huddle like little piles of rocks. They cling to the mountain streams. One of these is the old place named Mucurubá, a ghostly sight.

The mountain village is dark. It is as peaceful as death. Or sleep. For it is too cold to be out when the sun goes down in the Andes. On the road that silently winds through the village there is a dim light in a cafe, but there seem to be no lights anywhere else.

A man on a horse has ridden his mount into the doorway of the cafe. Several men in *ruanas,* the capes of the Andean Indians, have surrounded the rider. They seem to be arguing with inaudible voices. And suddenly, a man who is standing in the doorway of the cafe reaches up, and seizing the horse's reins, pulls the rider toward him, in a flash of anger, and punches the horseman on the chin.

The man is small in stature, as Andean Indians tend to be, so his feat is all the more remarkable. It is not easy to hit a mounted rider on the chin.

"*Bueno!*" I say. My friend silences me. On the Llanos, so he says, when the *llanero,* the cowboy, is insulted he often curses you with gusto. But, he is more likely to laugh than fight. Like most Venezuelans he enjoys conversation more than confrontation.

Not in the Andes. The Andean man is quiet; he seldom curses, but when he does he is usually deadly serious. If his name is insulted he will defend his name not with words, but with his fists, or worse. That is the old Indian way, my friend says: "One's word is like a stone. So be careful where you throw it."

"The men of the mountains are like the mountains," Señor Vincent says. "And they are hard as stones." More than anywhere else, the Andean people do hold onto their traditions. And they honor the old ways of thinking and behaving; they are as conservative as they are stubborn in politics and religion, in manners and talking.

Some of these villages are so far from the twentieth century that even now few roads can reach them. The old burro trails defy the new vehicles with four-wheel drive. In their huts of mud and stone the villagers see television with fifteenth century eyes. Nothing changes in the mountains, they say, but the days of the year.

"Ah, it is not true. Once this was the Tibet of America, but it is no more," my friend says.

"Why not?"

"Man changes everything," he says. "In the mountains it simply takes a little longer."

That night I sleep in Mérida, the Andean capital. It is the sleep of the fallen snow in the tropical night. And, in the morning, I awake in another world of dreams.

* * *

Once there were people who prayed to the mountain gods. For thousands of years they climbed the steepest slopes and clung to the narrow ledges and fell and struggled upward again. And they sent their priests to seek the highest peaks, into the shadows of the sun, in the hope they could touch the fingertips of the mountain gods and grasp the beginning and the end of time. But, that was before the invention of plastic backpacks. So they never touched the fingertips of the mountain gods.

And where are the people who prayed to the mountain gods? Where have they gone? They are sitting at home watching documentaries on television of mountain climbers atop the Andes.

And where are the mountain gods? Nowhere to be seen.

* * *

Of a graceful Spanish design, the wrought iron grill on the front door is charming and ominous. It is a guard against the crime wave of burglaries that have begun to terrorize the suburbs of the Andes. Between the bars the majestic crest of *Pico Bolívar,* Mount Bolívar, rises nearly seventeen thousand feet into the clouds; its glaciers are glistening in the morning sun.

"Is that Mount Bolívar?" I ask.

"There is no other mountain," my host says, "for us."

Morning has come. And I am awakened in a suburban house in a subdivision of the ancient city of Mérida, where the University of the Andes was established in 1634. It is a city in a mountain valley so high that the sky hovers over the television antennas and the peaks of the mountains touch the sun.

"Lord, what a sight to wake up to," I exclaim.

"Ah yes," sighs my host. "Every day we see the mountain at our doorstep. But, one morning we will wake up and find that a developer has built a condominium across the street. The mountain will be hidden by a high-rise building."

The modern house in these suburbs of the Andes might as well be in Chicago or New York; its chrome, electric kitchen is as anonymous in its efficiency as anywhere else in the world, and its carport is indistinguishable from any along the freeways of Los Angeles. But, the scenery is magnificent.

"Here? They won't build a condominium here," I say.

"Of course," he answers. "The scenery in these mountains is very expensive. Soon someone will sell it."

The suburban houses are separated by high walls, so the neighbors cannot see or talk to one another. If the children, who a few years ago roamed the high meadows in the mountains play with pebbles and sticks, as rural children do, they have to throw their pebbles and sticks over the high walls, for there is nowhere else to throw them. And their toys become missiles that crash loudly on the roofs and through the windows of the neighbors' unseen houses. It is safer for the children of the suburbs to play in the streets if they are to escape the anger of their neighbors. Even the banana trees, in the suburban backyards, are not for the children to climb. They too have become a part of the scenery.

"Ah, you see, we have not only urbanized the children," says my friend. "We have urbanized the banana trees. Soon we will urbanize Mount Bolívar."

"Nonsense," I say. "No one can urbanize the Andes."

And he smiles sadly, with an indulgent smile, at my naive and romantic faith in the strength of the mountains. "I hope not," says Señor Vincent.

* * *

Colonial buildings upon the plaza look like a film set. They seem perfect. If the ancient walls and the century old roofs of Jaji appear as though they were built a few years ago it is because they largely were. The government has restored the village plaza to all its original antiquity. And the town high in the Andes has been declared an historical site; it is as if Machu Picchu, the mythical city of the Incas, was rebuilt and repopulated with real people.

One by one the tourists come over the mountain passes to seek the history of their country. They are not foreigners, entirely. They come from the new cities and have undertaken the arduous journey, as pilgrims do, to see if the memories of their ancestors have disappeared from the countryside, as they have done in the cities.

In the quiet village where history has been reconstructed, they photograph one another before the newly painted and immaculate white church with its blue cross; purchase souvenirs made, not in Japan, but in Guatemala; eat in the "authentic" restored Village Inn; and pay one bolívar so their children may ride a real donkey on real cobblestone streets. It is somehow like an eagerly awaited, but ill-at-ease, visit to a distant relative whom one recognizes only from an old photograph.

"Sometimes we feel like actors on a stage," a villager says.

The village of Jaji is not a theater. Nor is it Machu Picchu. It is simply a place where Venezuelans go to see if they still exist.

People in the village go on about their lives from day to day, ignoring the tourists. In the country stores the merchants sell beans and cornmeal and herbs and Pepsi-Cola. And when twilight has fallen on the Andes the families all gather round their television sets to watch "El Kojak."

On the cobblestone streets behind the plaza there are three aging donkeys braying in protest against whatever fate awaits them. The butcher's shop is near the corner. In his narrow shop there is a modern refrigerated case, for his meat, that is covered with brown wrapping paper to shade it from the sun. And on the meat case there is a bloody axe, a large axe such as woodsmen use, which the butcher uses to cut up his carcasses. On that axe there are hundreds of flies. No, there are thousands. The butcher does not curse at the flies. Even a fly, he says, has a right to live. If he can.

Marcel, the butcher, is a fastidious man; his brown suede hat is set sedately on his gray hair. His moustache is neatly trimmed. It is a thoughtful moustache. And though he speaks with some emotion, there is the calm of wisdom, or perhaps merely resignation, in his voice. On this morning he seems to be unnecessarily philosophical. As do all small businessmen, he too speaks of the problems of being a small businessman. Nothing seems to interest him as much as his own doom.

"Our village is dying," he laments. "All the villages in these mountains are dying. The tourists from the cities come to see what our life is like, but we have to go down into the cities to earn a living. Everyone goes away.

"My own son will not work for me," the butcher says. "He has left the town for the city, for Caracas. There is no one to help me here. My own son is gone. In the city he is not doing well and I have to send money to him. But, he wanted to go. There was nothing for him to do here, he said. There was no money here. But, I think there will be nothing for him to do in the city. Nothing worth doing."

Suddenly, the butcher is merely a father. His complaint is universal and generational. "All the young people want to go to the city. They all want to have the pocketful of money. But, can everyone be a teacher or a technician? Someone has to work with their hands. If they do not how will the teacher and the technician eat?" The butcher shrugs at this modern absurdity. "Who will cut the meat?" he says.

"No one wants to work with their hands anymore. Even in this little village, where there are many without work, no one will work with me, no one. I have to work alone."

Jaji is a poor town. But, it is not so poor as a *barrio* in the city. There is a sense of dignity in the streets. There are no beggars.

And, I say this to the butcher. "If people do not work, how do they live?"

"Families eat together," he replies. "In the old days families worked together. The father and the mother and the children would all pick coffee together. And they could make a living. Now, the children have gone away and the father and mother cannot make a living. One person earns maybe twelve bolívars, three dollars a day, picking the coffee. They say that is not enough money. So they go to the city. They say they cannot live without money. But that is not so!"

On Marcel's face the lines about his eyes seem older than his eyes. He squints into the distance, as if he cannot see too well. "When I was a young man we had a terrible drought. Everyone was hungry. No one had any money.

People worked in the fields just for food. And then they took some of the food to the stores and traded it for clothing and things. So, they did not need money, you see. They needed only to work. That is the country way. In the city, you cannot do that."

Those days are gone forever, the butcher says. And they will never come back. Never, he says, will his son return from the city. And he knows that he must go on working alone. Until he dies.

He says: "One animal at a time, that is all I can slaughter with my hands. If I buy two or three animals, I must keep them in a pasture. There is no more slaughterhouse in the village anymore. Once there was, but the government inspectors came and closed it. They said it was unsanitary. So we have to send the animals down to Mérida to be slaughtered. That is a big city and we poor people cannot send them there. So, I have to slaughter them myself, with my hands. But, I am an old man. When I die who will do the butchering here? There will be no one."

For the first time, he laughs. He wipes his bloody axe. "Who knows. Maybe they will build a *supermercado,* a supermarket, in the village. They can use the church. It is big enough. And it is always empty."

A little boy comes running down the narrow street. He takes the reins of a donkey and leads him to the plaza. "The tourists! The tourists! They are here!" he cries.

Soon after he has said this the tourists will come to the butcher shop. Not to buy his meat, but to take a picture of this village man with his Andean hat and his bloody axe and his memories of days gone by. He will not pose for them.

* * *

On the campus of the University of the Andes, in the city of Mérida, upon the bulletin board of the faculty of geography, there appeared this poem to Mount Bolívar. It said in part:

> Colossal rock!
> Once so clear and remote
>
> Even now the pollution
> demolishes and darkens
> your snowy gift
>
> And your frozen rain
> falls like dry tears
> that are too parched
> and sinks into the sea.

Rivas Davila, the poet, has dedicated these lines to his fellow students of "nature's dialectics." He has named his poem "The Omen of Mount Bolívar."

Old Man in the Mountains

The old man had not come down the mountain in forty years. So we had to go up the mountain to him. He lives in a small house that is miles beyond the last paved road. In the past there was no way to visit him but on a burro, inching along the sheer cliffs, foot by foot. The old man's house is perched so high on the slopes of the Andes that from his veranda he can see the entire world below him. And he looks upon it with the bemused tolerance of an old goat, or a god.

On his veranda he greets us with a courteous bow. He waves three chickens from a nearby bench and then he bids us to be seated while he pulls up a broken chair with uneven legs, as though it is a throne. Somehow, with his baggy pants and jacket too large for his bony body there is something Chaplinesque about the dignity of his poverty.

In the village they say this old man knows more about life and death than anyone else, for he is the oldest man in the Andes, hereabouts. He is so old that he speaks to Simón Bolívar in his dreams. And he has seen all the governments rise and fall, the dictators come and go, the politicians born and die. In his lifetime he has seen the candles go out and the electric lights go on. And he remembers the day when the first automobile came into the Andes; it was on the first Monday in August, 1916.

So old is he that he says: "I know the silence that existed all over this world when Octavian Augustus ruled Rome; an extraordinary silence."

On coming into the mountains I had asked to see the wisest man in the whole country, someone who could tell me what has happened to the soul of Venezuela and of South America in these times when the old ways seem gone forever and the tempo of the times is set by the politics of computers and machine guns, and the passions voiced by the roar of bulldozers and oil refineries. No one seems to bow as courteously to guests as the old man has just done, and I wish to know why.

My friend who has taken me up the mountain is an in-law of the old man; the family of his wife grows coffee on these slopes, as the old man has done all of his long life. And he tells the old man that I have come from far away, in the United States, to ask him this question. The old man eyes me suspiciously.

And this is what he says: "Once this happened to old Solomon. He asked a man: 'By what letters can one summon the heart, when one needs it?' The man said, but remember he was evil: 'You know the five thousand languages. Take each language and place it in the fountain. Take the pens and dip them into the fountain, and the words will tell you everything.' But, wise Solomon broke all the pens and left. He said: 'There are no wise men upon this earth. There is no wealth. There is no wisdom.' I think this is how Solomon saved himself, because he had already lost heaven and who knows, maybe even God. So wise Solomon saved himself by breaking all the pens.

"No man can reach your heart with words," the old man says to me. I believe this is what he meant, for as I was soon to learn, he talks in parables that seem those of a scholar, though I am told that he has never gone to school.

Seeing that his words have saddened me, the old man smiles. He attempts to apologize. And so he says: "God gave everyone a power. That is why we all possess nine doors to the outside world. There are five doors that are easiest to open: our two eyes, two ears, and one nose. What do you call that? The five senses? But, the four other doors are harder to open to the world. One man whom I know, only one, who was given the gift of God, who knew it, who worked with it, and who used it successfully, was Leonardo da Vinci. Everything he did, he did through the nine senses. That is how you are going to write this book."

And yet, it is clear that he does not believe I am wise enough to learn to do this. So many people have come to these mountains through the centuries and have asked questions about the meaning of life but have learned nothing.

The old man is just a poor farmer. He is not a prophet. "I have never had a teacher," he says, "so I have to read in my head." All that he knows is what he has learned on his coffee farm. "I have never gone anywhere," he says. "You have traveled. But, I have just been sitting here on this mountain. I was born here, and some day I will die here." He philosophically scratches his scrotum.

On the walls of the veranda, where the coffee beans are dried in the afternoon sun, the three chickens are strutting like acrobats. Several little chicks try to imitate their parents, but one by one they fall off the walls and disappear, as if they had fallen off the Andes.

"See that?" the old man says.

"What?"

"You see! It is necessary to have a teacher. Even for a chicken."

Still, these strangers come to see him. Why do they keep on coming? Because they cannot remember anything. They do not know how to listen. And they do not know how to sit still. Even Moses was in a hurry and dropped the tablets.

"Tell me," I say to him, "why do these strangers behave this way?"

"It is because they are the 'Children of the Wolf,'" he says. "You know about the 'Children of the Wolf?' Let me tell you about them." And he does.

"Once there was a *cacique* who lived in the Land of Tiber. It was not yet called Italy. The *cacique* spent his time buying men and women, as slaves. And one day an Israelite sold the *cacique* a girl, named Rhea, and a boy named Antonio. After paying for them, the *cacique* asked the girl about their religion. And the girl said they believed in one God, the Father, who was King of Heaven.

"'No! That is a false religion,' the *cacique* said; 'There is no one who is better than the Goddess Diana.' You see, this *cacique* was like an Indian. 'But,' the girl said, 'I will die before I change.'

"So, the *cacique* got mad and put her and the boy into a dungeon. There he gave them water and wine. And he put a thief in the dungeon with them. In three months the jailer saw the girl was nursing two babies, who were beautiful.

"'How did that happen?' the *cacique* asked.

"'She gave birth! And she baptized them with the water you gave her,' said the jailer. 'One is named Romulus and the other is Remus.'

"And the *cacique* called his executioner and ordered, 'Take those boys from her and kill them in the Tiber.' But the executioner did not go to the Tiber. He went to a fig farm.

"There he left the boys. He did not kill them. Instead, he climbed a mountain and he found some flowers, as in a garden, and there he left them. Some shepherds found the boys five years later. These shepherds had gone to the mountain looking for a wolf that was attacking their sheep. And they found the two boys hanging from the neck of a wolf on the mountain.

"When the *cacique* heard about this he ordered his men to arrest them. Remus was caught, but his brother, Romulus, freed him. And they returned to the ranches of the shepherds, in the mountains, where they lived. And when someone asked the boys who they were, they would say: 'We are the Children of the Wolf. Our Father was a rogue, he was evil, but our Mother was a Saint.'"

As the old man talks, he stares at me; he stares straight into my eyes. He seems to be looking for a sign, if not of comprehension, then of recognition, as if he is telling me my family history.

"My name is Nicolas Vielma!" he says fiercely, as if to say: "And who are you? Are you one of the 'Children of the Wolf'?"

"That was a long time ago," I say to him. "And the world has changed."

"No," he says. "It still has the same thought. Even the Italian, Christopher Columbus, had to leave Italy to find the answers to his questions. He had to come to this country. It is not the world that has changed," he says. "It is the people who have changed."

And he says: "When I was born, everything was different. Everything was more backward, in one way, and fuller in another. But, it is not really so different because the world still has the same thought. My thought is like this. When you are born, you are in a cradle. No one pays any attention to you and you are just playing. From the age of ten you start getting involved in love here and there. At twenty you are dancing. You go out into the world and come back. At thirty when you come back, the wife comes out to meet you with two or three kids. At forty you are just there, with your arms open, and you have seen everything and arranged everything. Before you are forty you look for a good girl and dance and get married, and after forty everything goes downhill, downhill.

"Now, I am old. I am a little sick. My sight is failing me a bit. I have a bladder ailment. I have two fractures of my bones. But, I will not go downhill. I still move and work.

"Now, what I have been thinking is that the closer it comes to your time, the better life looks. Sometimes, when I talk, it is like dancing, precisely, as though I am dancing."

The old man is not quite ninety. He is only eighty-eight, he says proudly, if not defiantly. Still, there seems to be a physical vibrance in him which is not merely the vigor that an old man may feel when he is excited by his own rhetoric. He radiates a physical heartiness and strength.

I ask him: "Aren't you ever envious of the people in the cities? Those who can do so many things you cannot do on your mountain? Those who have become rich, while you are so poor?"

But, he dismisses the thought with not so much a shrug

as a grimace. "The rich who I have met are the same as me. Do they not eat food and sleep with their woman? To be rich you have to have the ambition to take it away from another. So you may be paid in rocks. Money makes you suffer," he says emphatically.

The old man pulls his chair closer to me. He leans forward importantly. Now I have the feeling that our talk is about to end. What he is about to say to me must have a special meaning which he wants to make sure I hear, even if I do not understand.

And he says: "One night I began to have a conversation in the room where I had gone to sleep. It was a dream. And in my dream there were people who were talking foolishly and I told them so and they wouldn't talk to me. But, I could talk to them all night because I had so many things to say. They wanted to talk nonsense, but I told them to listen to me because I possess everything in my head.

"In my dream I talked to Simón Bolívar. Don Simón was a gentleman, you know. He was a teacher and he was not so very innocent. One day he left here and he walked far away and he started spending money as if he were rich. And a journalist who saw what he was doing wrote to him that there is nothing wrong with having fun, but the way he was going was the way to being ruined.

"And Bolívar answered: 'Now I remember. You have made me a teacher of great things.' So together they went to Italy, where they sat down, all sweaty, by those pieces of marble, which were worn by time, at the Five Columns of the Children of the Wolf. He, Bolívar, walked back and forth, and he said: 'Here the Caesars lived. Here, they had the world and the people at their feet. Now the day will come when the New World will get even with them.' He spoke like that and then he sat down and he repeated the words twice. Then they left Europe. And they came back here.

"Bolívar had a dream in my dream. He said: 'I come wrapped in the robe of Eros. I visited the Amazonian fountains. I went to the watchtower of the Universe. I wandered, but the voice of Gran Colombia beckoned me to plead for the freedom of man. I walked and walked and came unto these great hills and here the spirit of Chimborazo guided me and I stood upon the threshold of the Abyss. From there, I saw all the plains of the Andes. I learned about all the hills and valleys. I watched where the Orinoco is born, whose waters flow in the shape of the vulva of a woman. I was standing here, thinking about these things when an old man appeared. He was very old and he was holding a sickle. He said this to me: "Oh, Child! Oh, Man! Oh, King! Do you think the universe is the head of a pin, that you can climb so easily to the top? Surely you know that I am the one who with one finger writes your destiny. My possessions are infinity. With my head I can touch eternity. With my hand the universe. For me there are no tombs, because I am greater than death. My mother is eternity and my brother infinity. Go, and tell your fellow men what you have seen and heard. And if they are democratic, go and lift your arms in their defense."'"

The old man stands up. He pushes back his broken chair. In the shadow of the portal, along his veranda, he begins to walk back and forth, like Bolívar in his dream, restlessly, and he begins to talk with a distant voice, as if he is talking to the mountains and not for me.

"From here one can see everything," he says.

"But, where do the mountains lead us? Where the water and the wind? Where the fire? And how do we know which of all these things sustains us?

"Who knows?" he says. "Who knows anything?"

And he turns to me, the weariness of his years in his eyes, peering at me with a pained compassion. He offers me his hand. The bones are surprisingly hard and firm, but his grip is gentle and lingering. He is sending me away, unhappy that our talk has had to end.

In his eyes there is a querulous curiosity, as if to say: "Can you understand anything I have told you? Have you learned anything at all?"

That is not, however, what he says to me as he waves goodbye and our jeep inches its way onto the burro trail in its precarious journey down the mountain to the valley. He says with a smile: "When you come back bring me something pretty that you have written." And I know that if I do, he will take my words and will retell them as he does with the words of the Bible, the Romans, the Andes, the Venezuelans, until they become part of the folklore of the mountains. Even now, I know from his eyes, my coming has become a folktale the old man is retelling in his mind.

The Night the Jaguars Were Let Out of Their Cages

On the night that I came to this country someone had crept into the darkened zoo in the city of Mérida, high in the Andes. The man, whom the newspapers called the "lover of animals," had opened the door of the cage of the jaguars. And two of the caged animals had escaped into the night. In the city, the morning after, there was no panic. The marketplace was crowded and the traffic did not diminish and the children played a new game called "jaguar."

The man who had opened the cages of the jaguars had left a note. It said: "These animals are not being treated with dignity. So I have freed them."

And in the city it was said: "The jaguars have gone home to the mountains. No one can live in someone else's cage." One man said to me: "That man, he did not free the jaguars. He has freed himself. It is not the Venezuelan way to live in a cage."